· LANGUAGE AND POETRY OF FLOWERS ·

A flower presented with leaves on its stem expresses affirmatively the sentiment of which it is the emblem; stripped of its leaves it has a negative meaning: if the plant be flowerless, the latter is expressed by cutting the tops off the leaves.

When a flower is given, the pronoun *I* is implied by inclining it to the *left*, and the word *thou* by inclining it to the *right*.

If an answer to a question is implied by the gift of a flower, presenting it to the right hand gives an affirmative, and to the left a negative reply.

The position in which a flower is worn may alter its meaning – on the head it conveys one sentiment, as *Caution*; on the breast another, as *Remembrance* or *Friendship*; and over the heart a third, as *Love*.

If the flower be sent, the knot of the ribbon or silk with which it is tied should be on the left as you look at the front of the blossoms, to express *I* or *me*; and on the front *thee* or *thou*.

A SELECTION OF FLOWERS WITH THE POETICAL LANGUAGE
——— EACH IS SUPPOSED TO CONVEY ———

Auricula (scarlet) *Avarice*
Blue Bell *Constancy*
Carnation *Woman's love*
Chrysanthemum (red) *I love*
Chrysanthemum (white) *Truth*
Crocus *Gladness*
Daffodil *Chivalry*
Daisy (garden) *I share your sentiments*
Geranium (ivy) *I engage you for the next dance*
Geranium (silver leaved) *reversed decision*
Hyacinth (blue) *Constancy*
Hyacinth (purple) *Sorrow*
Iris (yellow) *Passionate love*
Jonquil *I yearn for your affection*
Lavender *Distrust*
Lilac (white) *Purity*
Lily of the Valley *Promise of happiness*
Marigold (French) *Jealousy*
Myrtle *Love in absence*

Orange blossom *Your purity equals your loveliness*
Orchid (Lady's Slipper) *Capriciousness*
Pansy *You occupy my thoughts*
Peony *Anger*
Phlox *Our souls are united*
Rose (deep red) *Bashful love*
Rose (dog) *Pleasurable but painful love*
Rose (white bud) *Ignorance of love*
Rose (yellow) *Declining love*
Rose (red and white in conjunction) *Unity*
Snowdrop *Consolation, hope*
Sweet Pea *Departure*
Sweet William *Gallantry; finesse; a smile*
Tulip (red) *Declaration of love*
Tulip (yellow) *Hopeless love*
Violet (blue) *Faithfulness in love*
Violet (white) *Innocence, modesty*
Zinnia *Thoughts of absent friends*

5-27-94

Marypat,

Country Garden

The Kiss of the sun for pardon,
The sound of the birds for mirth,
One is nearer God's heart in a garden,
Than anywhere else on earth.

Love, Holly

THE
VICTORIAN
FLOWER GARDEN

The Victorian FLOWER GARDEN

JENNIFER·DAVIES

W•W•Norton & Company
New York   London

ACKNOWLEDGEMENTS

I am deeply grateful to each person who has given up time to talk to me and to everyone who has loaned reference books.

I thank Roy Cheek for his kind advice and help, especially with finding plants.

Thank you to my editors, Heather Holden-Brown and Deborah Taylor, for their guidance and invaluable support.

For professional photographs I thank Robert Hill and for skilfully uniting such illustration with text, designer Linda Blakemore.

I acknowledge with appreciation the kindness of the late Colonel John Ward and continued interest and kindness of Mrs Elizabeth Ward and Captain Gerald Ward.

As always, I am indebted to Harry Dodson, Peter Thoday and thank Keith Sheather and everyone involved in making the television series *The Victorian Flower Garden*, for without it, there would not be this book.

Copyright © 1991 Jennifer Davies
First American Edition, 1992

All Rights Reserved.

ISBN 0-393-03100-4

W.W.Norton & Company, Inc.
500 Fifth Avenue, New York, N Y 10110
W.W.Norton & Company, Ltd.
10 Coptic Street, London WC1A 1PU

Printed in Great Britain

1 2 3 4 5 6 7 8 9 0

CONTENTS

·

FOREWORD

The Victorian Flower Garden completes a television and book trilogy which is based on life and work in Victorian gardens and kitchens. As with *The Victorian Kitchen Garden* and *The Victorian Kitchen*, this book seems to have grown naturally out of Jennifer Davies' work as Associate Producer and ardent researcher of the television programmes.

I have been lucky enough to have been associated with all three television series. As part of the production team, I identify closely with them. But I have discovered that being involved in filming and script-writing within your own professional area is a frustrating business. So much must be left out, not simply through lack of programme time but in order to improve the quality of the films. I was consoled by the thought that Jennifer would be able to expand some of the stories.

However, by cleverly blending her first-hand observations of Chilton Foliat's head gardener Harry Dodson with her exhaustive readings of his nineteenth-century predecessors, Jennifer has produced a book that is both a celebration and a portrait of the craft of gardening. Rarely do horticultural studies of past glories dwell on the day-to-day activities of gardening; nor do they record and reflect, as Jennifer Davies has done, on the life of the working gardener. Hers is a picture of the doing and the doers, of the work and lives of the people who lived in both the bothy and the head gardener's cottage.

Her distillation of a formidable pile of nineteenth-century books, catalogues and gardening magazines also reveals very clearly what a significant role flowers played in Victorian society and the central position they occupied in public and private ceremonies. Whether the focus of attention was bride or *belle* of the ball, floral decoration for the rich was lavish almost beyond our imagination. And the demands placed upon Victorian head gardeners by their employers were large. Commercial floriculture and the florists's trade were in their infancy and the bulk of a house's flowers had to come from its own gardens – those same walled gardens that produced a year-round supply of fruits and vegetables.

It is likely that many of you who have bought this book will also have enjoyed *The Victorian Flower Garden* series. I hope you would like to join me in thanking and congratulating everyone concerned. The television programmes allowed our interest to come into focus; Jennifer's book gives us a more permanent record.

Peter Thoday

INTRODUCTION

It's an odd word – 'salmagundi'. You don't often come across it in conversation and it isn't in my dictionary. It means a hotch-potch or chance medley. In the past two years I've met it twice, on the first occasion as the name given to a winter salad and more recently, in a small book where the writer warns against a 'salmagundi of gardening'. There is a connection between these two encounters: the salad recipe and the warning were both written in Victorian times when the word was common currency.

There is another more personal connection. The salad salmagundi was included in a BBC television series called *The Victorian Kitchen*. In this Ruth Mott acted ably as a 'Victorian' cook and brought to life the recipes of a mansion kitchen. I had the pleasure of working with Ruth as part of the television team.

The Victorian Kitchen grew out of a previous series called *The Victorian Kitchen Garden*. In that, a walled kitchen garden had been planted with old varieties of fruits and vegetables and cultivated by head gardener Harry Dodson exactly as it would have been in Victorian times. In her Victorian Kitchen Ruth cooked the fruits and vegetables which Harry had grown.

Now 'salmagundi of gardening' comes into all this because it was mentioned in a nineteenth-century book on flower gardens, and I was reading the book to help with the research for our latest television venture, *The Victorian Flower Garden*. This new series was also fathered by *The Victorian Kitchen Garden* for that walled area of abundance didn't supply only kitchen produce. It had another equally important role, acting as a nursery and sometimes as a show place for the countless flowers and plants which Victorians loved and used to decorate their homes and fill their flower gardens.

In *The Victorian Flower Garden* Harry Dodson, who is as equally at home with flowers as he is with fruits and vegetables, lays out flower beds with nineteenth-century varieties of flowers and puts back into use a stovehouse for exotics and a 'show house' for year-round floral displays. He also creates a Fernery (a Victorian obsession); 'forces' flowers out of season; makes up wedding and ball bouquets; decorates drawing rooms, dining rooms and ladies' boudoirs with flowers and does countless other tasks expected of a Victorian head gardener.

Harry was not quite alone in doing all the above. Always he had the

Previous page: The Stove House at Chilton brought back to Victorian splendour

A century ago mansion flower gardens were tended by a more fulsome workforce. This old photograph shows merely the pleasure-ground men, additional gardeners worked at flower production in the walled kitchen garden

support of his wife, Jane. Then there was David Aplin fresh from college and anxious to learn methods of flower cultivation which no modern curriculum teaches. I think he found it hard work sometimes, particularly the weeding and watering of the herbaceous border which was 110 feet (33.5 m) long and 10 feet (3 m) wide – twice over, being in two sections either side of a pathway, but it always looked immaculate. Harry also had the support and comradeship of Peter Thoday who presented the television series and helped viewers explore such delights as a Fern museum in Barnstaple and a Victorian Violet nursery brought back to life after a hundred years.

This book is a bit of a salmagundi. It is partly about how we reconstructed the garden for filming; a lot about flowers and plants in Victorian times and quite a bit about Harry, who must now feel as old as Methuselah having been made 'Victorian' three times!

Jennifer Davies

CHAPTER ONE
The Bedding Craze

*Tadpole Flower Beds – Bedding out – Perplexing shapes – Ribbon borders –
Tired gardeners – Making the Clematis bed – Spring bulbs –
Leaving the Lesser Celandine.*

'Unmeaning flower beds', which looked like 'kidneys, and tadpoles, and sausages, and leeches, and commas', profoundly upset the early Victorian writer of an *Essay on the Poetry of Gardening*. He blamed their existence on the 'picturesquians' who, although their day had gone, still seemed to linger on in garden parterres.

The offending picturesquians were members of the Picturesque Movement whose aim was to make the landscape look natural – in fact more than natural; they wanted it to look as it might best be seen in a picture, requiring that it should have the same piquancy for the eye that a painter sought in the spirit of his picture. Their quest began as a reaction against the classical or Italian style of landscape popular in the eighteenth century. In this symmetry had been everything. The central line of the mansion had been carried on into the formal geometric gardens and echoed in the parklands by an avenue of symmetrical trees.

By the time of the kidney- and comma-shaped flower beds, and despite other 'irregular masses' still being fashionable, the more excessive piquancies of the Picturesque (such as the introduction of dilapidated cottages and other ruins into the landscape) had somewhat abated, and by the middle of the nineteenth century Robert Kerr's *The Gentleman's House or How to Plan English Residences* was happily advocating a mixture of classical and picturesque (or English) style for most residences: 'A certain amount of symmetry is almost invariably adopted in the best examples for the immediate adjuncts of the House; while as regards the more remote arrangements the English style is now exclusively employed.'

In fact, the laying-out of classical Italian gardens with terraces, formal flower beds, balustrades and flights of steps had become positively fashionable. The popularity of these architectural gardens had been helped on its way by a new method of flower gardening. It was called 'bedding-out' and was considered to be a convenient and striking way of filling formal beds. The practice owed its origin to the introduction into Britain in about 1830 of brightly coloured annuals, mainly from the west coast of America. Subsequent hybridised versions of these annuals, too tender to withstand the rigours of a British winter, had to be kept under cover, but in early summer, with the danger of frosts past, they were bedded out into the garden.

Bedding-out plants represented an exciting novelty. They provided bright, all-over, long-lasting colour in a flower bed. It was something the old sorts of garden flowers had never totally achieved, for during the greater part of the summer many perennials were just stems and leaves.

The ability to have instant and constant colour for a third of the year led to the vogue for arranging flowers in sheets of one colour. The effect was striking and brilliant. It was known as 'massing', and, writing in the *Journal of Horticulture* in July 1872, the Reverend C. P. Peach believed that he could almost date the advent of its popularity to the introduction of two flowers: 'Purple King' Verbena and a scarlet Geranium called 'Tom Thumb'. 'Tom Thumb' came to prominence in 1845.

Indeed, scarlet Geraniums and purple Verbenas, along with yellow Calceolarias, were among the most popular bedding plants. Each amply fulfilled the desire for brilliance, denseness and duration of flower and, with a little help from improvers, they were made legion. For example, of Calceolarias it was said that perhaps no plant had ever been hybridised more extensively, a fact which led to one writer of the time stating in mock despair: 'And what, in the name of moderation, is one to do with four thousand new seedling, shrubby Calceolarias, all named varieties, beautiful as they doubtless all are?' Of Geraniums, following improvements to make scarlet ones dwarf so that they sat better in flower beds, the first pink-coloured varieties made an appearance in about 1845 and rose-coloured ones a year or two later. From the middle of the nineteenth century work began on perfecting Geraniums with bands of three colours in their leaves. A beautiful variety called 'Mrs Pollock' which, despite selling for 3/6d a piece, three times the price of other variegated-leaved Geraniums, became a favourite. It had leaves with green centres circled by a band of bronze-red which in turn was surrounded by a deep edging of gold. Writing in 1870, garden journalist Shirley Hibberd attributed the ability to obtain such tricolour beauty as 'the most conclusive evidence obtainable of the power of art to alter the course of nature'.

Art, helped by the bright and constant colour of bedding plants, was also altering flower beds. There was for some gardeners, however, a black spot on the palette – a worry. It was over how best to group such an abundance of colour in order to create that Victorian acme of garden

Previous pages: A Victorian family in their Italianate style garden at 41 King Edward Road, Hackney

taste, a 'harmonious whole'. To help attain this, certain canons were laid down. Geometrical flower beds were considered ideal for displaying bedding and instructions were written to help gardeners design them. Mrs Jane Loudon, in her *Ladies' Companion to the Flower-Garden*, recommended using paper covered with regular squares, like the sort containing plans for Berlin worsted-work. Another optimistic garden writer came up with the comforting prediction that, given a few evenings' practice with a ruler and compass (and, presumably, the appropriate squared paper), a gardener could produce an endless variety of plans. For those with a bent towards mathematics this may have proved the case, but an entry in the *Journal of Horticulture and Cottage Gardener* for 1861 confirms that such accomplishments were by no means given to all. It seems that in their attempts to cut three oval beds in a lawn (each oval being required to 'vary accurately in its proportions relatively to the others') a group of gardeners failed completely and the owner of the garden had to ask the village schoolmaster to come and mark out the beds.

At least these perplexing flower beds had been oval. Had they been shaped like stars or diamonds, that same owner might have had continuing difficulties for, according to the same *Journal* (albeit at a slightly earlier date):

A gentleman with a lady on his arm walking amongst flower-beds full of sharp points, is in one of the most unenviable positions one can imagine. The lady's attention is so taken up with the flowers, that she is in danger of treading on these sharp points at every turn; and he, poor man, must keep his eye on these 'points' to save the lady from, perhaps, a tumble down.

Below: Diagram from the Irish Farmer's Gazette *showing the harmony of colours ·*

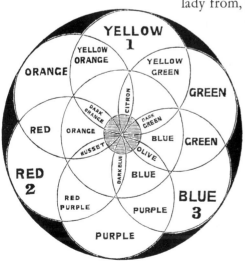

With the shape sorted out, the quest for a harmonious whole in the flower garden could be furthered by a proper understanding of how to fill the beds using harmony and constrast of colours. Again, written advice on this was ample. Even the *Irish Farmer's Gazette*, which seems an unlikely organ for such aesthetics (although one may be doing it an injustice), carried a diagram illustrating the harmony of colour. As to how to ascertain their contrast, David Thomson, gardener to Lady Mary C. Nisbet Hamilton at Archerfield in East Lothian (1868), supplied a useful method in his *Handy Book of the Flower Garden*. He cited the experiments of M Buffon who had discovered that if a wafer was placed on a white sheet of paper and gazed on steadily for a few seconds,

*Left: The Geranium
'Mrs Pollock'*

Right: Harry Dodson

when the eye was moved to another part of the paper a spectrum of the same size as the wafer and in its contrasting colour could be seen. Buffon's spectrum theory revealed the following as contrasting:

Black	– White	Green	– Reddish-violet
White	– Black	Blue	– Orange
Red	– Green	Indigo	– Orange-yellow
Orange	– Blue	Violet	– Blueish-green
Yellow	– Indigo		

Once the principles of harmony and contrast had been conquered, it could be understood that harmonising colours like red, dark pink, pale pink and white, placed in that order, presented a gentle and beautiful transition 'something like a plaintive melody in music'. Mixing harmony and contrast was thought to be equally effective. For example, a yellow centre with a corresponding zone of white finished off with a fringe of blue. The two centre colours harmonise, while the blue contrasts.

Another finding was that the most accommodating colour for contrasting with others was white or very light grey. Thus plants of these colours became popular as edging material. The *Floral World and Garden Guide* of March 1868 particularly recommended *Hedera helix Marginata* (silver-variegated ivy). This does indeed sound wonderful for apparently, in addition to its merits of being chaste, sparkling and neat when viewed from any standpoint, if trained left and right and pegged down, it would form 'glittering silvery lines'. By contrast these would brighten considerably any scarlet or purple flowers that they encircled. Without the need for training, but perhaps with equally startling effect, were ornamental Minton tiles which some garden owners employed as edging.

However, going back to Mr Thomson and overall harmony: to avoid any jarring to the eye he believed that geometric designs should have corresponding beds planted up not only with the same colours but with the same plants too. Advice of this sort must have contributed to the colossal number of bedding plants of the same colour being favoured in gardens. Yellow Calceolarias and red Geraniums were planted in so many beds that complaints of sameness and eyes being tired from the glare of bright colours began to appear in garden journals. Significantly some of these complaints came from head gardeners and it is small wonder, for to meet fashion the amount of bedding plants needed (one calculation put the number at 100,000 for a single good-sized garden) and the work such plants involved was phenomenal. You were, as one gardener put it, two thirds of the year preparing what would give pleasure for just half that time. This preparation involved keeping up stocks by each year taking thousands of cuttings and putting them into pans or boxes to make root. In winter the cuttings had to be sheltered to keep them free from frost and damp. Room had to be made for them in the pits and glasshouses of the kitchen garden. This was a sore point with gardeners, for they needed all available glasshouse space to force pots of potatoes, peas, dwarf beans and wooden trays of salading in order to keep the mansion kitchen supplied throughout the winter months. By February the young bedding plants were large enough for each to be potted on into a 3-inch pot. Every week these pots would need going over, particularly those containing quick-growing Calceolarias and Verbenas, for any plants that were outstripping their companions in growth had to be pinched back. A look-out had also to be kept for greenfly on the leaves, and if any were spotted, the plants were fumigated with tobacco smoke. Finally, before being planted out into their summer flower beds, the plants had to be hardened off. This meant finding sufficient space, neither too hot not too cold, in which to stand them out until they were ready.

In addition to all the work which cuttings involved, gardeners were also obliged to over-winter one-year-old bedding plants, for these would become profuse with bloom in their second year. This is where Harry Dodson enters the bedding story. Harry distinctly remembers how, sixty or more years ago, when a remnant of the bedding-out style was still practised in private gardens, Fred Norris, head gardener to the Earl of Selborne, dealt with the problem. Harry's memory is particularly sharp on this because Fred Norris was his uncle and Harry, from the time he was knee-high, became unofficial garden boy at Blackmoor Gardens in Hampshire. Uncle Fred, he says, had tiers of wooden planking made and placed in the 'late' fruit houses. These were the vineries and peach houses where the heating was sufficient to keep the frost out but not high enough to start the trees or vines into growth. In fact, the temperature was ideal for over-wintering the pots of one-year-old Fuchsias, Calceolarias and Geraniums which, once placed in rows on the tiered planks, continued to bloom happily. It was, says Harry, a good way of keeping them, for by using the tiers you could accommodate far more pots in the house than you would have had room for on the floor and as a bonus they brought something every head gardener sought, a focus of interest and a talking point for visitors. There was only one slight drawback that Harry remembers, perhaps because of his size at that time – watering the top shelf was difficult.

It is doubtful whether Uncle Fred would have experienced the excessive extension of the bedding-out craze which took hold in the

1860s and 1870s (which is just as well as even his tiered staging couldn't have coped with it). This was for the ribbon border, which consisted of bedding plants running along a border in a number of broad uninterrupted lines. Ribbon borders often meant the demise of old herbaceous plants still lingering, for it was their border which became transformed.

In 1870 John Robson, head gardener to Viscount Holmesdale at Linton Park, near Maidstone in Kent, had, along with his other flower beds, to fill two ribbon borders which each measured 593 feet (180 m) long and 10 feet (3 m) wide. In his own estimation these borders were the equivalent of 150 circular beds of 10 feet (3 m) diameter. Describing the borders in a horticultural journal, Robson admitted that, owing to his flower beds having 'multiplied so much faster than the structures capable of accommodating them', he was forced to plant out directly from cutting pans and boxes, fortunately without adverse effect.

Lack of proper facilities to cope with bedding plants bedevilled most establishments. The problem was attributed to owners who, on seeing great bedding displays in their neighbours' gardens, expected their head gardeners to produce the same but without giving them proper houses or additional help. Gardeners complained of the weeks spent watering and moving plants and, in some cases, of having to trust to candlelight to 'master the potting shed'. Some men, having potted until after midnight, never went to bed at all for fear they would be late at their post in the morning.

In among all this angst one bedding plant appeared which didn't need half the administrations given to its fellows. Being a hardy perennial it didn't need to be over-wintered at all. It was Clematis, in particular the rich violet-purple *Clematis* 'Jackmanii'. It became a bedding plant by accident. At Woking a firm of nurserymen called George Jackman and Son were specialising in Clematis, an expanding business for, increasingly in the nineteenth century, new varieties of the plant were being introduced into Britain by plant collectors. Using these, particularly the ones brought from Japan and China, and crossing them with existing sorts, nurserymen like the Jackmans managed to produce Clematis with rich deep colouring, in some cases with flowers measuring a remarkable 9 inches (23 cm) across. *Clematis* 'Jackmanii' had been raised by the Jackmans in 1858. This is Mr George Jackman's version of its conversion to a bedding plant:

> It happened that some of the plants in the plantation of hybridised seedlings from which C. 'Jackmanii' and others were selected, were blown down during the early part of the summer, and the poles not renewed. As the summer and autumn passed on, it was noticed that

these plants spread out their branches over the surface of the ground, and flowered as profusely there as when elevated in the usual way. It was thence inferred that, if pegged down like Verbenas, the varieties of Clematis would make good bedding plants, while they would have this advantage over ordinary bedding stock, that they would be permanent, flowering year after year, and that with increased vigour as they became more thoroughly established at the root.

Although we had not attempted the intricacies of ribbon borders, the idea of a beautiful glowing (and, it seemed, easy to maintain) bed of Clematis was distinctly appealing and so Harry set forth to make one.

Engraving of a Clematis bed taken from a Jackman's advertisement

As assistance he had a helpful book, published at Jackman's nursery in 1877 and called *THE CLEMATIS AS A GARDEN FLOWER: Being Descriptions of the Hardy Kinds of Clematis, with Select and Classified Lists, Directions for Cultivation, and Suggestions as to the Purpose for which they are adapted in MODERN GARDENING.* The book had obviously left nothing to chance. But even the most seemingly comprehensive can err.

To show the Clematis plants off to their best advantage the bed had apparently to have a convex surface. Several methods of attaining this raised look were listed in the book. Harry opted for what seemed the simplest one, pegging down a layer of twiggy branches. It so happened that, rather like at the time of the Clematis' metamorphosis into a bedding plant, there had just been a gale. Deposed twiggy branches were thick on the ground. Perhaps it was their abundance, together with the book's lack of information as to how many actually to use, which led at the end of one afternoon to the bed sporting a substantial thatch. It looked impressive but the Clematis plants found it hard to work their way through to grow over and, what with the incredibly dry summer and a few marauding rabbits ready to snap up any stray shoots, the bed was not a glorious success. Indeed, had Harry been a real Victorian gardener, I think he would have been tempted to implement Mr Jackman's recommended winter covering of the bed at an extraordinarily early date. This was to plunge pots of small bushy hardy evergreens into the bed, the object being to overcome the appearance of baldness given when the Clematis died down. These pots were extracted in March as the Clematis began to grow again.

Victorian gardeners also used pots of dwarf evergreens to fill the beds vacated in winter by the more orthodox tender bedding plants. The method brought a lot of labour because the evergreens had to be kept waiting in the wings, watered and shaded all summer. At the first sign that the tender bedding plants had been touched by frost they would be whipped out and in a day the beds be replete with evergreens of varying foliage colour, planted strategically to give contrast within the beds. Such niceties of contrast weren't sought by all, however. Some garden owners preferred their beds left empty to present harmony with the general aspects of winter.

Victorian aristocrats were often at their town residences during the spring and early summer and it was for this reason that the gardeners at their country mansions tended to neglect spring flowers and put their energies into producing large amounts of late-flowering summer bedding. As such families were the arbiters of fashion, this neglect of spring flowers spread to the flower beds in gardens of smaller houses where the owners stayed in residence all year. However, from the late 1860s the planting of spring flowers began to gain in popularity. They were planted in October and removed in time to make way for the summer bedding.

The Duke of Rutland's garden at Belvoir Castle in Leicestershire was held up as a fine example of what could be done. A visitor to Belvoir in the spring of 1868 eulogised over the quiet beauty of the flowers there.

Common Primrose (double-flowering)

To his surprise they included many common plants such as Primroses, Aubretias, Pansies and Daisies. They gave plenty of colour but weren't gaudy and tiring to the eyes like summer bedding.

This delicacy of colour plus the fact that many spring flowers were sweetly scented (an attribute most summer bedding lacked) helped establish the vogue for spring gardening.

One method of obtaining spring flowers was to prepare perennials and annuals beforehand in a reserve plot or in the kitchen garden: for example, growing rows of Primroses in trenches like those dug for celery. However, the bulk of spring gardening consisted of planting bulbs such as Tulips, Crocus and Hyacinths. Nurserymen began to increase their lists of these and were rewarded by brisk trade. The most prolific users of spring bulbs were parks. In 1877, as well as extensive

An 1880s' nursery catalogue shows the delights of a Spring promenade

HYACINTHS AND TULIPS IN REGENT'S PARK—SUPPLIED BY CARTERS.

beds of Tulips, Hyde Park in London was noted for having oblong beds of early Hyacinths, one variety to a bed, running the entire length of Park Lane.

On a less grand note there is a spring flower which Harry remembers and which goes back years. He has a clump of it at his cottage, in a border which faces south looking towards the River Kennet. It is Lesser Celandine. Harry says that old gardeners used to leave Celandine and not weed it out; for one thing the little bulbils were too small to remove easily and for another it was tolerated with affection. It was a spring weed that gave a welcome splash of yellow at a dull time and very obligingly died down after flowering.

CHAPTER TWO

Sub-Tropical and Carpet Beds

*Sub-tropical bedding, a troublesome affair – Roland Rat helps with a carpet
bed – Walking the plank – Succulent beds – Mrs Ralli's matchless bed.*

 As in the first quarter of the nineteenth century a movement
had been active to promote tadpole and comma-shaped flower
beds in reaction against classical geometric ones, so in the second half of the century a similar battle was waged against
bedding-out. Protestors complained about the strong, flat and
monotonous use of colour and their offered alternative
became known as the 'sub-tropical movement'. In this tender, statuesque, tropical plants were removed in early summer from the confines
of the glasshouse and planted out into open ground. They occupied beds
or were placed singly with the pot plunged into turf. The latter method
was thought to be particularly picturesque, although care had to be
taken, for too many isolated single plants could appear 'dotty'.

The acknowledged king of sub-tropical bedding was the superintend-
ent of Battersea Park, John Gibson. He constructed beds with a foundation of broken bricks which were supposed to have a three-fold benefit:

*Sub-tropical gardens in
Battersea Park*

they afforded drainage; trapped atmospheric air and gave height to soil placed on top of them. Given height, the beds caught the sun, and if the weather turned cold their make-up ensured that the heat they'd accumulated was lost slowly. Anyone needing ideas on how to set about sub-tropical bedding was urged to visit Battersea Park, and the following glowing report was written in the *Journal of Horticulture and Cottage Gardener* of 20 August 1868:

> There, just now, may be seen noble-leaved Bananas and Palms. India rubber plants and Indian shots (Cannas) in profusion, Coral plants, Dracaenas, Caladiums, and groups of handsome Tree ferns, whose thick black trunks offer a unique feature in an out-door garden in this country . . . The luxuriance of growth which the more tender exotic plants exhibit this year is remarkable; they are no starvelings, but tall specimens, some of them, the Bananas for instance, with leaves 8 to 10 feet [2.4 to 3 m] long; indeed, persons who have seen them in their native countries affirm that for beauty the specimens at Battersea are much superior, and for size nearly equal to those seen in the natural habitats of the plants.

Fired by such an example, there were some gardeners bold enough to carry out and succeed with tropical bedding as far north as Scotland. One reported planting out such exotics as Bananas, Caladiums and Dracaenas in his garden in Kirkowan. The only problem experienced was some damage from high winds. To counteract similar damage, gardeners even in the comparative warmth of the south chose sheltered dells for sub-tropical beds. Harry remembers that when he was a general foreman at Nuneham Park near Oxford there had been such a dell there, although the sub-tropical plants had long since disappeared.

Another desirable condition was a solid background against which to show off the finely cut foliage and elegant shapes of these summer migrants from the garden hothouses. When Harry came to demonstrate the art of planting a sub-tropical bed, such a background presented itself in the form of a yew hedge. This hedge surrounded a sunken garden at Chilton, near Hungerford, the estate where, until his retirement, Harry had been head gardener for forty years. The site was particularly pleasing as it fitted in exactly with diagrams in late Victorian gardening books. These showed collections of sub-tropical beds planted to the left of mansion fronts, obviously to be admired by the resident family and by visitors as their carriages swung round the final bend in the drive before arriving at the front door.

It proved a difficult and cumbersome task getting several large Palm trees, not to mention tall Rubber plants, three even taller *Sparmannia*

A noble-leaved Banana (Musa cavendishii)

africana, several less tall Fatsia and a startled-looking Banana plant, all complete with pots, the half mile or so from the kitchen garden. Harry said that years ago the head gardener would have used the garden's pony and a small wagon. There had been a garden's pony when Harry first came as head gardener to Chilton. It lived in a paddock some distance from the stables. Harry knew it by name only, for although it was always referred to as 'the garden's pony', the creature, advanced in years, never graced the garden with its presence. In fact, when it eventually died Harry was quite relieved because it meant that he could have a van.

Despite the lack of conventional conveyance a motley group of plants eventually arrived on the stretch of ground in front of the yew hedge.

It must be admitted that, once in place, the Palms, with their pots sunk into turf at isolated intervals, *did* look interesting. They formed a sort of spartan jungle adjacent to the large round bed into which Harry carefully disposed the other tall plants. Once these were in position he put, at intervals beneath them, variegated Aspidistras, quite striking in appearance. Finally he covered any remaining bare earth in the bed with a pattern made from a mixture of silvery green and dark-red-tinted Echeveria.

The lady of the house, passing on the day after the bed was planted, was moved to remark that the assemblage looked 'extraordinary'. It did too, until a particularly windy spell played havoc with the frail pale green leaves of the Sparmannia and leant the Ficus out at a dangerous angle.

Below: Sparmannia

Below right: The wind begins to whip through Harry's sub-tropical bed

The most vulnerable had to be removed and given temporary refuge in the sunken garden behind the yew hedge.

The sub-tropical bed turned out to be a troublesome affair for, on the fine days when Harry wasn't worrying about wind or rain damage, he was concerned about the amount of water the plants needed to stop them flagging. Unlike Mr Gibson of Battersea Park, who had had a plentiful supply of water 'distributed with the greatest ease, by means of hose on small wheels', Harry had no water supply within convenient distance and it all had to be hand-carried.

Harry's experiences bore out the bad press which, despite their stately beauty, these sorts of beds had gained among his Victorian predecessors. Latterly gardeners had attempted to make beds less vulnerable by introducing what were much hardier but, it was hoped, equally picturesque plants; one writer dubbed this 'sub-arctic' gardening. Indeed, Harry, who deep down is really a fruit and vegetable man, would probably have preferred the sub-tropical look suggested by the *Floral World* (1868). Among Yuccas and Aspidistras it recommended placing edible gourds; *Crambe cordifolia* (a giant species of seakale); a potato called 'Chardon' with blue flowers; crimson-leaved Beet; Indian corn; and Angelica.

Roland Rat, cartoon rodent, proved the hero of the hour when Harry came to lay out an example of the next fashion to arrive in the Victorian flower garden.

In order to complete some part of Roland's anatomy, Bath City Council's Parks Department, who are past masters of three-dimensional floral design, had grown copious amounts of a small creamy-yellow-leaved succulent called *Mesembryanthemum cordifolium Variegatum*. Harry needed some of this – in fact, a fair bit – for a 'carpet bed' design we had spotted in Cassell's *Popular Gardening* (*circa* 1880 edition). The Parks Department kindly agreed, hopefully not at the risk of making their rat look mangy, to let Harry have several boxes.

Carpet beds surfaced, rather literally, in Victorian gardens around the 1870s. The *Gardener's Chronicle* for 8 October 1870 remarked of them: 'Lately another style of bedding has sprung into existence and one which bids fair to take the public taste.' How they achieved their name isn't clear. It may have been because the first ones were perfectly flat, like a carpet on the ground. Or it may have been that some of the intricate patterns in which they could be planted up looked like those on Turkish carpets.

The ideal situation for a carpet bed was on or below a formal terrace where it could be seen through the drawing-room windows or, better still, looked down on from the upper floor of the mansion. The patterns worked in such a bed were made up not of flowers but of the coloured leaves of various dwarf plants; hence the quest for the creamy-coloured Mesembryanthemum. Many plants used had the added novelty of being recently introduced into the country. In fact an article in the *Villa Gardener* of December 1876 describes *Mesembryanthemum cordifolium Variegatum* as being 'new' and a 'decided acquisition in decorative gardening'.

As time-went on, in order to relieve the overall impression of stiff formality the beds presented, a few standard graceful-foliaged plants were added. This extension of the style became known as panel gardening. Some people, because of the exclusion of flowers, thought carpet beds too artificial. There were others, however, who delighted in the way the small coloured plants could be used to make intricate patterns, and beds which spelt names, displayed coats of arms or quoted mottoes were soon to be spied beneath mansion windows.

The carpet bed pattern

The carpet bed pattern we'd chosen in Cassell's didn't aspire to anything as complex as the above but it was complicated enough. It was like a flower which had six petals joined by an outer rim. The whole had to have a raised edging of *Herniaria glabra* (green). Then between the lines numbered as follows there was to be a groundwork of: (1) *Sedum glaucum* (greenish-grey); (2) *Alternanthera amabilis Latifolia* (a mixture of green and red); (3) *Mesembryanthemum cordifolium Variegatum* (creamy-yellow) and a central plant of *Echeveria metallica* (greyish-purple); (4) *Lobelia pumila* (dark blue); (5) *Pyrethrum* 'Gold Feather' (bright yellow-green); (6) *Coleus blumei* or *Iresine lindenii* (dark red/wine); (7) central plant *Dracaena australis* (a shock of spiky leaves like a fountain) surrounded by *Centaurea candidissima* (silvery white).

The diagram gave the carpet bed as 20 feet (6m) in diameter but as the quantity of plants needed for this would have been astronomical (bearing in mind how closely they need to be planted), it was decided to go for a bed half that size.

Next came the quest for the plants. The *Herniaria glabra* Harry grew from seed (in excess of 500 plants). *Sedum glaucum* proved elusive and so we substituted blue-grey Echeverias (estimating for 1000 plants, a mixture of Harry's propagation and ones purchased). *Alternanthera amabilis Latifolia* (introduced from Brazil in 1868) had a reputation for being difficult, and indeed Harry was surprised at the amount of heat needed to get the young plants into growth, so we ended up with a belt-and-braces mixture of both Alternanthera and the more amiable, purple-coloured Ajuga (over 350 plants). *Mesembryanthemum cordifolium Variegatum* came, as already explained, courtesy of Roland Rat (1200 plants). The *Echeveria metallica* required as a central 'dot' plant among the Mesembryanthemums didn't appear to exist any more, so at a friend's inspired suggestion purple-black *Aeonium atropurpureum* were substituted (6 plants). *Lobelia pumila* had disappeared and so Harry grew copious boxes of *Lobelia* 'Crystal Palace' (dark blue and of the same era). He also grew some *Pyrethrum* 'Gold Feather' from seed and others came, already in plant form, from Cannington College of Horticulture in Somerset (about 600 plants); Pyrethrum, being relatively hardy, has the merit that it can be taken up and passed on. The Iresines were grown from cuttings Harry took (180 plants). And, finally, there was the *Centaurea candidissima* (32 plants) taken from cuttings.

Harry got the soil in the 10-foot (3-m) bed almost as fine as flour. Any lumps would have made it difficult to mark out the pattern. They'd also have caused problems at planting time by disrupting the desired overall smoothness. He formed the soil into a slight dome so that the pattern the plants formed would show up well.

Meanwhile the diagram from the book had been transferred with the aid of a compass to a sheet of graph paper. Armed with the sheet of paper as a guide, Harry then had to substitute pencil and compass for several thin stakes and a length of rope and attempt to mark the design on to the bed. Tying a length of measured rope to a central stake and fixing the other end to his 'drawing' stake, he drew the outer circles. Then, by judicious placing of the other stakes by the same method, he drew a series of arcs and cusps which turned into the six 'petals' of the design. The centre circle was easy – just a case of shortening the rope on the central stake.

Freshly scratched aside, the soil of the lines was darker than the rest of the bed, but in the heat of the day it would dry and the lines fade. To avoid this Harry tipped a thin trail of sand along each line. Eventually the pattern lay clearly etched over the bed.

With the aid of the garden's wooden handcart it needed two or three people to gather up the seedtrays of young plants. Some trays were in glasshouses, others had commandeered a whole row of coldframes, and there was a sizeable army of minuscule flower pots, each containing a stud-like rosette of Echeveria, standing in lines on the kitchen garden terrace. A stout plank and two logs (of equal size) had also to be added to the load. Once they had been transported to the marked-up bed, the order of planting was for the centre or 'dot' plant to go in first. Getting to the centre of the bed to do this without treading out the lines of the pattern was a delicate operation. As planting got underway a log placed at the top and bottom of the bed and a plank stretched from one to the other, proved a precarious but efficient planting platform. By moving

Above: Harry scores the carpet bed design onto the soil

Above right: A trail of sand defines the lines

the logs every so often, the platform could be adjusted as planting progressed.

David Aplin, Harry's young assistant, did most of the planting. Harry's advice to David was to keep an eye forward and not over-plant in one spot with any particular plant in case the supply of it ran out. David proved a fast and able planter and, when he'd finished, far from having run out, he had a fair number of plants left over. The bed looked truly stunning. Seeing the surplus plants Harry felt a tinge of regret that we'd not been bold enough to attempt the original 20-foot (6-m) design. It may have been a blessing in disguise that we hadn't, for at regular intervals the bed had to be clipped all over to stop the plants becoming rank and spoiling the pattern. It was a time-consuming task and meant either Harry or David (mostly the latter) crouching on the plank platform with a bucket in one hand and a pair of sheep shears in the other. The shears might have been old-fashioned but they could be operated with one hand. It seemed a pity to have to keep the Mesembryanthemums cropped because, left untouched, each would have borne a delicate pink flower. The *Herniaria glabra*, needed to be clipped – not on top but at its edges – as it grew naturally flat on the ground and would have spread itself into the lawn. In fact this particular plant turned out to be a surprise. In its wooden trays it had looked like an insignificant weed, but planted out there couldn't have been a better edging for the bed. It formed a delicate, green, feathery ring, a foil to the

Left: David Aplin (right), helped by fellow gardener John Lawson, gathers up plants needed for the carpet bed

Below: Harry starts the planting off by inserting the Dracaena australis

Right: Once planted, the bed had to be clipped regularly to keep it neat

Below: A bird's-eye view of the clipped bed

more upright bedding plants it encircled and a pleasing transition from them to the surrounding grass.

The only plant to cause slight problems was the Lobelia, which looked sad and lop-sided after rain. This was a pity for the blue panels gave richness to the pattern. In retrospect it was easy to see why the original instructions had recommended a dwarf Lobelia like Pumila. By contrast the lines of Echeverias remained crisp and unperturbed whatever the weather. It was understandable (departing briefly from carpet beds) that whole beds were sometimes devoted to Echeverias mixed with similar impacable plants such as Sempervivums and Sedums. Such amalgamations were known as 'succulent beds'. Any dullness of hue was thought to be offset by the succulents' curious and picturesque shapes.

Interestingly grotesque as they may have been, few succulent beds could have competed with the carpet bedding at Cleveland House, Clapham, London. Writer and gardener David Thomson was favoured by one Mrs Ralli with seeing such from an upper floor of her mansion. He recorded the event in the 1876 edition of his *Handy Book of the Flower Garden*. Looking down to a circular lawn at the foot of a terrace, he saw 'almost matchless carpet beds'. These, one circular and six oblong, were raised a foot (30 cm) above the level of the lawn and each had a gentle slope upwards towards its centre. Such was their perfection that he was moved to write: 'In these beds – a border 60 yards [55 m] long by 8 feet [2.4 m] wide, and a few minor beds – upwards of sixty-thousand plants are arranged, and there is not in carrying out the designs one plant too many or – such is their completeness – one too few.' The gardener at Cleveland House had obviously 'kept his eye forward' when planting, but one wonders whether at the expense of such precision he too, as the last plant was put into place, found himself surrounded by a perplexing surplus.

CHAPTER THREE
Herbaceous Borders

*How herbaceous plants came back in fashion – Harry and David replant Mr
Beckett's herbaceous border – A Buttercup causes disgust – Wendy's
Delphinium – Frost – A Sweet Pea screen – Peonies – Mr Beckett's brother's
Michaelmas Daisies – Setting a plant alight – The 'pretty opening'.*

Along the back wall of the kitchen garden at
Chilton there is a row of the usual appurten-
ances necessary to the endless production which
takes place within the garden. The row starts
with the (now empty) pony shed and progresses
along past a boiler house to two vegetable forcing houses. Needing darkness to accomplish
their purpose, the forcing houses have no windows and their outer walls link to present a solid
mass of brickwork which stretches unrelieved
until it reaches a neat white window frame. This
window lets light into the head gardener's
office. Inside, a desk is immediately below the window, a necessary
placement, perhaps, because of the smallness of the room but nonethe-
less, for lighting purposes, economic.

Such economy is, however, partially eclipsed by pride and sentiment,
for hung in the centre of the window directly above the desk is a square
picture frame. It contains an aquatint so faded that it needs Harry to
voice in the details. It is, he says, a fine old picture and shows the herbaceous border laid out by Mr Charles Beckett, head gardener at Chilton
some ninety years ago. The border was, as Harry discovered when he
became head gardener, a difficult one to plan and bring to perfection,
for on her ladyship's orders it had always to be in the family colours
of blue and light straw yellow. Despite this and the added handicap of
having to have the herbaceous border in full bloom at a certain time –
the end of July and the first twelve days of August, before the family left
for their home in Scotland – the abundant pale shapes in the picture
looked blooming and overflowing.

Mr Beckett had made the border run either side of the central walkway which led north to south across the 4-acre (1.6-hectare) kitchen garden. To have a floral display of such importance in the kitchen garden
might seem odd but it was a legacy of the time when bedding plants

ruled supreme in the gardens around villas and mansions and when for the most part herbaceous plants existed only in the kitchen gardens of the rich and the cottage gardens of the poor. No doubt the herbaceous border flanking the kitchen garden at Chilton had for the majority of Queen Victoria's reign been a far simpler affair than the blue-and-yellow showpiece it eventually became.

The return of fashionable interest in herbaceous plants had been gradual. It was helped by a number of factors. Chief among these was the decline in the popularity of bedding-out, for despite its merits of having brought flowers within the reach of all – for example, huge bedding displays in parks which could be enjoyed by the 'lower orders' and the availability to the middle classes of bedding plants at local nurseries – the system began to pale. There were numerous reasons for this. It was found to be expensive and labour-intensive to carry out on a large scale, and those who had not the means but still wanted a grand display brought the fashion into disrepute by using inferior plants. Criticism began to be voiced that bedding-out flowers were vulgar and gaudy and cautionary papers were written on how to combat the problem by increasing the variety of plants used and avoiding large beds of primary colours. Added to all this there was dissatisfaction among some garden owners that spring bedding had to be pulled up while still in flower to make room for summer bedding. For those who didn't practise spring bedding this wasn't a problem, but then they had their own problem of empty flower beds during spring. Capital was made of this latter state by the horticultural journalist William Robinson, who wrote:

> I never was more struck with the utter folly of the bedding system, as usually carried out, than when passing through a road of some fifty first-class villas, after a day's ramble amongst the woods and lanes in the neighbourhood of Sevenoaks towards the end of March. The cottage gardens were all ablaze with Primroses of half a dozen colours, Violets, Pansies, Daffodils, Crown Imperials, blue Anemones, purple Aubretia, and white Arabis, and the woods and lanes were equally bright with Primroses, Violets, Cuckoo flower, and Wood Anemones, as thick as they could find standing room in many places. The villa gardens, on the contrary, were a blank, and showed no more signs of spring than they did at Christmas.

To combat such blankness Robinson urged the planting of a mixture of hardy bulbs and hardy perennials.

The above anecdote comes from *The English Flower Garden*, published in 1883. This book contained, as Robinson acknowledged in the preface,

Right: Part of the herbaceous border at Chilton

a large amount of information he had obtained from the pages of his journal, *The Garden*. Robinson had begun to publish the journal in 1871 and used it as a vehicle to promote hardy herbaceous plants.

In the same year that *The Garden* was founded, herbaceous plants received a boost from another quarter. The former manager of the Herbaceous Department at Kew, William Sutherland, brought out a book called *Hardy Herbaceous and Alpine Flowers*. The object of the book was, he said, to give people a better knowledge of 'these neglected plants'. They had been so long banished from gardens that he believed even those who had been practising gardening for thirty years knew little about them. In his book Sutherland did not condemn bedding-out if it was done well but stated that he saw a place in all gardens for mixed borders. Such borders, he believed, should have a broad groundwork of hardy herbaceous plants mixed with annuals and bedding plants so that the whole looked effective throughout the year. He pointed out that a mixed border gave as much scope for taste and skill as bedding-out but was less costly and, as an additional benefit, 'the individuality of the plants is not altogether swallowed up in the general effect.'

All this renewed interest was fuelled by the fact that hybridists and seed raisers had improved many herbaceous plants. There was also more choice than earlier on in the century as new sorts had been introduced from overseas. One further circumstance helped raise their popularity. The Parcel Post started in August 1883 and this, together with a spreading network of railways, enabled people to purchase good, cheap plants from reputable nurseries.

Happily possessed of the requisite hardy plants, gardeners faced decisions as to their planting. It was acknowledged that such plants *could* be grown in beds in grass, but it was generally thought that they looked more attractive for the owner and his friends if grown in large borders.

New fashions arose as to the laying-out of these borders. In the old 'mingled' type popular before bedding-out took hold, tall plants had always been put at the back and others placed in front in descending order. Now the system was less formal, with the sloping angle being broken by the introduction of some tall plants near the front. Formerly plants had been placed in single file at regular distances from one another and the spaces between them kept as bare earth. The new mode was for plants to be massed in groups so that their colour could be appreciated from a distance. Any spaces between groups was carpeted with low-growing plants.

Colour in herbaceous borders became the speciality of an artist, Miss Gertrude Jekyll. In 1898 she and Mr H. Selfe-Leonard were asked to contribute plans of hardy-plant borders to the journal of the Royal Hor-

Above: Gertrude Jekyll

Above right: The Rev. S. Reynolds Hole

ticultural Society. They contributed three plans. In plan 1, flowers bloomed from May till September. In plan 2, flowers bloomed from spring till the beginning of August (useful for establishments where owners quit at the end of the London season and went to their country houses). In plan 3, flowers bloomed in late summer or autumn (useful for country seats). In the opinion of Miss Jekyll and Mr Selfe: 'It is obvious that a border planned for all or many seasons can never be as full or as brilliant during any one of them as can a border furnished for one season alone.'

Writing in *Our Gardens* (1907 edition), the author S. Reynolds Hole acknowledges that it must be delightful to realise the masses of bloom and contrasts of colour and form that these three plans gave, but 'for those who have neither the science nor the supplies, I think that a mixed collection, planted according to knowledge with reference to size and colour, would give the larger amount of pleasure.' It was Reynolds Hole's sort of border with pioneer William Sutherland's ideas mixed in which Harry designed, although in a roundabout way he did have some help from Miss Jekyll.

Overleaf: The herbaceous borders in mid-summer

Harry's Victorian herbaceous borders were on the site of Mr Beckett's – that is, they ran either side of the main walk of the big kitchen garden. The only trace left of the glories of the former borders was not in the soil but on the gravel walk. Half-way down this, standing in the centre of a large bird bath raised on a plinth, a fat stone cherub solemnly held a bunch of stone grapes perpetually to his lips. The cherub had been standing on the path when Harry came to Chilton in 1947 and had probably been there a long time before. In fact, he may not have actually been on the path the very day that Harry arrived for, as in good gardening tradition, Harry took over the gardens at Michaelmas (29 September). September was always the first month of the cherub's confinement to winter quarters to avoid his becoming cracked by frost. In the spring he made his reappearance, in four parts on a special trolley made by the garden's carpenter. The trolley was fixed with a tripod and a windlass which helped hoist the stout bits of plinth. Harry recalls that this operation used to take two men, the bricklayer and his mate, almost all day.

Harry put David almost, but not quite, to double-dig the two borders, forking in large quantities of well-rotted farmyard manure. It was no small task, for each of the two borders were 10 feet (3 m) wide and 110 feet (33.5 m) long. Having decided on the old sort of mixed border, Harry didn't have the restrictions that he'd once endured of making the flowers match the family's colours. However, he had a greater handicap: because of the filming schedule for the television series he had just one year in which to make the borders look spectacular – an almost impossible feat as herbaceous borders look their best only after two or three years of growth. In order to telescope the natural time span he needed large chunks of root stock and crowns; the small equivalents sold in pots by garden centres would have been lost in the two vast borders. Few places have borders of such a size that they can afford to thin out large chunks in autumn and even fewer have plants which owe their place in the border to late Victorian fashion, but there was one and not at an impossible distance from Chilton – Hestercombe Gardens in Somerset. The gardens belong to the Somerset Fire Brigade, and head gardener Dave Usher maintains them as closely as possible to plans found in the gardens' potting shed. The plans were drawn by Miss Gertrude Jekyll when she helped Sir Edwin Lutyens design the gardens at the turn of the century.

Harry went to Hestercombe to look at the borders and, as goodwill exists between head gardeners and could be laced with a contribution to Fire Brigade funds, it was agreed that, when the borders were thinned in the autumn, clumps of various plants would be put aside for Harry. This

was a great relief, but until that time came Harry had no idea of the quantities he would get. In the meantime he had to plan his borders and found that being in the dark about how much he could expect from Hestercombe made it a difficult job to work out what was to be planted where and the distances to allow between.

In addition to the Hestercombe material Harry grew from seed a huge quantity of annuals and perennials. Before ordering the seeds we used Sutherland's *Hardy Herbaceous and Alpine Flowers* as a guide to see what in the past might have been included and cross-checked the flowers it listed against those in modern seed catalogues. Some the old book recommended we failed to find at all. Where, for instance, was Willow-leaved Ox-Eye Daisy, introduced from Austria in 1759 and said by Sutherland to be 'an excellent mixed-border plant'? There were other gaps too, but we ended up with a good selection – in fact so many that, to save time, Harry identified them on the labels in the seedboxes by their seed catalogue numbers and not their names. He admitted that many he'd never seen in flower; for example, a few sorts of Poppies and a blue herbaceous Lobelia. One particular batch of seedlings he tended with great interest, their box, like others, merely identified by a number. On the day that I brought some old types of Ranunculus to the garden purchased from a specialist nursery in Devon, an odd expression came over Harry's face. He looked at the newly acquired *Ranunculus acris* 'Flore Pleno', which was a slender double Buttercup, and, turning on his heel, disappeared to reappear a few moments later holding a nicely potted-up plant from the box in which he'd taken particular interest. He compared the foliage of this with the Ranunculus, then, in exasperated wonder, informed me he'd just realised what his plants were – Buttercups. It was the first time that Harry had been called upon to cultivate common field Buttercups. On reflection I can't remember them ever making an appearance in the herbaceous borders. Perhaps they did briefly and perhaps David pulled them up, thinking that they were weeds.

Delphiniums, needed because of their height for the back of the border, proved a problem. Despite the fact that between 1878 and 1918 there had been a thousand distinct varieties introduced, none of the members of the Delphinium Society, after kindly taxing their brains, knew where any pre-1900 *elatums* (tall, stately types) could be obtained. However, a very kind lady member of the Society offered a *D*. Bella-donna delphinium (shorter than a *D. elatum*) called 'Wendy'. Wendy had overshot the Victorian era by quite a few years. She'd been bred in the 1930s. Nevertheless she is today an interesting rarity and was being kindly offered and so we very gratefully accepted. The lady who had offered 'Wendy' was herself called Wendy and, in fact, made a hobby of

Right: Drawing out where clumps will be positioned in the herbaceous border

Below: Almost, but not quite, double-digging

Below right: Sturdy Foxglove plants being positioned in front of paler-leaved Macleaya cordata. *The Foxgloves to bloom first and the* Macleaya *to take over from them*

collecting plants bearing her name. Wendy, both plant and owner, were in Kent, a considerable distance from the garden, but a neat plan was implemented to obtain the plant. Harry went to London to judge apples and pears at the Royal Horticultural Society's hall in Westminster. At the pre-arranged time of a quarter to eleven, after he'd executed his duty over the fruit, Wendy (owner), having recognised Harry, stepped out of the wings and presented him with two carrier bags, a 'Wendy' delphinium in each. These survived Harry's journey home and were eventually planted out mid-border, opposite the stone cherub.

When 'Wendy' flowered she was a stunning gentian-blue, flecked with purple. If Victorian improvers of Delphiniums had spent their energies in adding brightness to colour, Wendy was a fitting tribute to what they'd set out to achieve. She deserved her place in the border.

A taller plant, again sought for the back of the border, had not such a happy ending. Harry raised *Macleaya cordata* known to the Victorians as Bocconia or the Plume Poppy from seed and kept it along with other young plants in a coldframe until the time came for planting out. *The Garden* of 7 September 1878 referred to *Bocconia cordata* as 'a truly handsome and noble-looking plant, having elegantly cut foliage as large as that of the Fig, with the under side of a rich, shining, velvety hue, which, when seen upturned slightly by the wind, has a very striking effect'. Harry had chosen the plant because he intended that it should be planted between some Foxgloves and where it would take over from various clumps of Hollyhocks. It was, he said, 'one of the quickest things I know in the herbaceous line which will form a background for us'. Alas, it didn't. Within a few days of planting an extraordinarily hard, late frost decimated the young plants. The same frost also perished all the peach, nectarine, and most of the cherry and plum blossom in the kitchen garden. It was the first time for several years that, come summer, there wasn't a peach on the south wall.

Herbaceous borders benefit from a backing of some sort, one which filters the wind but stops strong gusts damaging the flowers. The rows of apple trees which had once framed Mr Beckett's border had long since been grubbed up and so a substitute had to be found. Old books suggested putting up screens of wood covered with ornamental climbers such as Clematis, Passion Flowers and Roses. Given time to allow the climbers to become established, this would have looked lovely. Harry didn't have time and so came up with an alternative. It was wood of a sort, a tall row of sticks cut from nut trees; one leaning against another so that the top of the row looked like a long spare line of wigwam tops. At the foot of each stick he planted an old variety of Sweet Pea called 'Painted Lady'. Its flowers are a mixture of pink and white and are

The Sweet Pea 'Painted Lady'

Above left: Delphinium *'Wendy'*

Left: Bocconia cordara (Macleaya)

smaller than those of modern Sweet Peas, but their fragrance is heavier. In among these he put another vintage Sweet Pea, also diminutive in its blue-mauve flower but again with a strong perfume. At the time of Harry's planting the identity of this Sweet Pea was unknown but it was later identified as Countess Cadogan. A 1lb (500 g) bag of its seed had been very kindly sent to Harry by Tom Acton, head gardener at Arley Hall in Cheshire. Although some might deem the deeply-coloured petals dull in comparison to those of today's light-coloured varieties, it had long been a favourite at Arley. Each year Tom collects seeds from the row he sows in the kitchen garden. The plant is not, to my knowledge, in the herbaceous border at Arley. That enormous double herbaceous border is unusual, for in the 1840s Arley's owner, Roland Egerton-Warburton, decided to plant it when, it seems, most other large houses were preparing to submerge themselves in the formal bright shapes of bedding-out. He and his wife Mary maintained it for over sixty years. For their descendants Tom has helped look after it for fifty years. It is well worth seeing. In recent times the gravel path between the beds has been grassed over. Gravel walks were thought necessary in Victorian days for (as one manual of the era points out) tender and delicate ladies 'who will not set the sole of their feet upon grass'.

Those with delicate extremities could traverse the lengths of Harry's restored herbaceous borders quite happily. A gravel walkway runs between them and ends at an ornate iron gate. The gate leads out of the southern end wall of the garden and into the outside world of the public highway. Harry had been forced some time previously to put chicken wire over the gate because it had proved too convenient an entry point for opportunist moles and rabbits. This was a pity because the wire masked the attractive ironwork. Harry said that the gate had always been known as 'the pretty opening' and was put there so that locals on their Sunday walks could peep through and enjoy the view up through the borders. With restoration of the borders under way it seemed a good idea to transfer the wire on to a portable frame the same size as the gate so that as and when the hoped-for view was due to be admired the frame could be put to one side.

If such admiration was to begin early in the year, certain plants would be useful in the borders. One was the Peony. Unlike in the case of the Delphinium there was still a choice of Victorian varieties available for purchase. It must be admitted, however, that the varieties of Peonies both old and new were not as numerous as they had once been. It didn't take too long choosing from the half dozen sorts offered in a modern catalogue but days would have been required to decide which were best among the 850 or so varieties Messrs Kelways of Langport were offering just under a hundred years ago. At that time Kelways were the largest growers of Peonies in the country and responsible for great improvements in them. An article in *The Garden* for 1874 sums up the transformation which was taking place:

> Vulgarity is the idea which has long been associated with the effects of the Paeonia; and, as regards the old roughly-formed, and glaring-coloured varieties, emitting odours anything but pleasant, the association may be correct . . . But there is a race of Paeonias now in cultivation which, for perfection of form and delicacy of colouring, vie with the queen of flowers herself, and many of them are sweet-scented. They embrace all the delicacy of colouring which lies between the pure white, the pale pink, the delicate blush, the brilliant rosy-purple, the crimson, and various other effective and pleasing colours . . . the flowers are as double and compact as the finest rose, and the blooms of great size.

Newly imported Peonies had helped swell the ranks of material available for crossings in order to achieve improvement and a fragrant species called *Paeonia albiflora*, introduced from Siberia, was used to give scent to many hybrids. The resulting perfume of some sorts was likened to that from Carnations and the finest Tea Roses.

In 1899 Kelways were rightly using the slogan, 'The Paeony is the FASHIONABLE FLOWER', and they had made it so. They helped spread the popularity of Peonies to the USA by exporting crowns and offering prize medals at large flower shows in New York and Boston. Evidence that such exporting continued is still pinned to a cupboard door at Messrs Kelways (who very kindly let me visit to look at their archive catalogues). The notice warns of disruption to shipping, no doubt to be taken into account when making up orders – world wars have a lot to answer for.

Harry planted four different varieties of herbaceous Peony, including one named 'Baroness Schroeder' which is very fragrant and dates back to 1888. He regretted that we had not purchased any Tree Peonies, whose size and beauty had made them increasingly popular in late Victorian gardens. There was, in fact, a Tree Peony already planted in the smaller of the two sections of walled kitchen garden at Chilton. For many years it had been by an archway which led from one kitchen garden to the other. This plant has a beautiful amber flower tinted pink at the edge of the petals. Each flower head is so large that when it opens its weight turns the face downwards. Harry's job was to turn up the faces and support them with slender sticks so they could be seen by the lady of the house when she visited the garden.

Paeonia albiflora

It being the intention that the borders should display colour well into early autumn, we purchased several *Kniphofia uvaria* (the Common Flame Flower or Red Hot Poker). Nicholson's *Dictionary of Gardening*, published in 1884, described it as the 'handsomest species in cultivation, and one of the most gorgeous of autumn-flowering plants'. As a foil to the coral-red and orange spikes of Kniphofia and with the capabilities of flowering from their name date (29 September) for several weeks, Harry was anxious to have a selection of Michaelmas Daisies. Such anxiety would have seemed strange to Eugene Delamer for, writing in his book *The Flower Garden* (1860), he described Michaelmas Daisies as 'great, straggling, gawky things, which would be disregarded, but that they put forth flowers . . . when almost everything else is in the sear and yellow leaf, and are therefore acceptable to help to fill up bouquets'.

Michaelmas Daisies laboured on under various other un-complimentary descriptions, such as drab and uninteresting, until late in Victoria's reign when one man set about lifting their appeal. He was Edwin Beckett, the brother of Harry's predecessor at Chilton, head gardener Charles Beckett, whose border we were bringing back to glory. Whereas Charles seems to have been a pleasant, even-tempered fellow, his brother Edwin was more fiery. He held a considerable position in the gardening world, publishing a book on vegetable culture and winning a record number of gold medals for his vegetable exhibits at Royal Horticultural Society shows. As head gardener to the Honorable Vicary Gibbs at Aldenham House, near Elstree, he had charge of between eighty and a hundred gardeners, one of whom, Arthur Pulham, I met by chance. It was on a day when I had been visiting Humberside to find out about an entirely different aspect of Victorian gardens. In talking to Mr Pulham I discovered that in the early 1920s, at the age of fourteen and a half, he'd started work in the gardens of Aldenham House under Edwin Beckett who was his great uncle. He clearly remembered Mr Beckett growing Michaelmas Daisies from seed and having trial grounds containing 2000 seedlings. He recalled how Beckett and the Honorable Vicary Gibbs used to spend hours checking and selecting from these. The ones they chose were put into the Aster border which contained two or three hundred Michaelmas Daisies. Each spring the plants in the Aster border had their shoots reduced to five and, with the use of five stakes, each shoot was trained out separately. Edwin apparently said that the finest example he ever bred was one he called 'Climax', which bore a tall, single, lavender flower. However, his then young great nephew remembers another with more interest. It had beautiful, double, lavender flowers and was called 'Robinson VC': Beckett had named it after the airman who shot down the first Zeppelin at Cuffley in the First World War.

Kelway's catalogue cover, 1898

Below left: Peony 'Madame Calot'

Below right: Peony 'Felix Crousse'

Above, top to bottom:
Aquilegia caerulea,
Aquilegia vulgaris,
Penstemon glaber

Above top: Malope trifida
'Grandiflora'

Above: Red Hot Poker

*Right: A Beechwood
Michaelmas Daisy*

Thinking that 'Robinson VC' (lovely though it must be, if it still exists) might seem a bit out of place in our Victorian border, we sought and were lucky enough to obtain earlier examples of Edwin Beckett's Michaelmas Daisies. Harry was kindly given some by a retired head gardener whose hobby is keeping old plant varieties going, and I received great help and a good selection of young plants from Paul Picton who has part of the National Michaelmas Daisy Collection at his nursery in Colwall, near Malvern. Among these were some deep pinkish-red ones known as the Beechwood varieties. Edwin Beckett had been the first to bring this colour to the *Novi-Belgii* species of Aster which most people know as Michaelmas Daisy. It also seemed fitting to have the Michaelmas Daisy which Edwin Beckett had named after himself, a silvery-white-flowered plant which bears its flowers in October and grows up to 5 feet (1.5 m) in height.

Harry had no delusions about the amount of planting, weeding and watering the herbaceous borders were going to demand – he knew that it would be considerable. It was, and more, because summer brought drought. In such conditions years ago he remembered the men under his uncle at Blackmoor Gardens supplementing their galvanised water bodges with 40-gallon (182-litre) barrels of water pulled down to the borders on a truck. Young David had it easier in that he could use a hosepipe but, even so, he wearied at the amount of hours he had to spend watering Harry's two borders. The hot, dry weather meant that many plants did not make the growth which Harry would have liked. It had been his intention that, come July and August, not a patch of bare ground would be visible in the borders and in order to achieve this he was forced to add more annuals and bedding plants than he would have done given normal conditions. But every cloud (even the white fluffy rainless sort that floated above the garden) has a silver lining, and these additions helped to make the now truly mixed borders a brilliant mosaic.

In retrospect the component parts of the borders are too numerous to list individually but I'd be at fault for not mentioning some. In the early part of the year Aquilegias had given the border delicate colour, in particular a tall elegant one called *Aquilegia chrysantha* 'Yellow Queen'. A brighter, tighter yellow was displayed by the miniature double Wallflower 'Harpur Crewe'. This sweet-scented flower gets its name from the Reverend Henry Harpur Crewe of Buckinghamshire who rescued it from extinction in the late nineteenth century.

The mosaic of the summer months was edged every so often with the bright, delicate petals of *Portulaca grandiflora*. An import from Brazil in 1827, this low-growing plant basked in the heat reflected up from the light-coloured gravel on the path. There were vivid patches of purple

Verbena venosa and, taller and less brilliant but still living up to its nineteenth-century reputation of being among the most handsome of ornaments of a mixed border, the common purple Loosestrife. Harry particularly liked the hardy annual *Eucharidium breweri*, better known as 'Pink Ribbons'. It had come to this country from California, probably in the 1890s. The Pink Ribbons made a marvellous display in the frames before planting out and were at their best in the borders in June.

Two plants which occasioned a lot of interest when visitors came were *Malope trifida* 'Grandiflora', the Mallow whose ancestors were introduced from southern Spain in 1808, and an import of three years later, *Penstemon glaber*. The Penstemon is a hardy perennial with an eye-catching mixture of blue and violet in its petals. Smaller than most of its kind, it reaches a height of about a foot (30cm). Much taller, the Malope filled mid-areas of the borders with large clumps of rose-coloured flowers; the outer sides of its petals shone like silk in the sunshine.

A plant which *might* have sparked off interest had it made sufficient size and flower was *Dictamnus albus*. Victorians considered it handsome in a border and it had another benefit, a singular peculiarity which they could turn into a party piece. This oddity was first noticed by the daughter of the eighteenth century Swedish botanist Linnaeus. By chance one evening, when she approached a *Dictamnus albus* with a light, a flame shot out of its flowers. This curious happening led many people to see if, by holding a lighted match close to a flower spike, they could get the same result. The success rate was poor until, in the summer of 1857, someone noticed that *Dictamnus albus* flower spikes bore minute reddish-brown glands which secreted an etheric oil and these were at their fullest when the flower was fading. A lighted match set against the flower spike in this state always met with success and caused a strong, reddish, crackling flame which, when it died out, left a heavy incense-like smell. The heat of the summer rendered our own *Dictamnus albus* too lacking in flower to enable us to try this, and anyway it seemed a shame to set into combustion so young and frail a plant.

At Michaelmas the borders presented a haze of blue and silvery-white Daisies with, every so often, the Beechwood pinks making a deeper splash of colour. Mr Edwin Beckett would surely have been pleased had he seen them so. His brother Charles would have been pleased too for, despite early spring frosts and the drought of summer, the borders would have reminded him of glories past. Harry also had reason to be pleased, because he'd achieved, as he'd intended, a show of flowers in the borders for many months. Indeed, those passers-by who had again taken to peeping through the 'pretty opening' must have thought that, chicken wire or no chicken wire, it had been a very good viewing year.

Dictamnus albus

CHAPTER FOUR
Wild Gardens

Wild Gardens – Harry's first job – Old Daffodils at Chilton – Peter Barr,
the Daffodil King – Flicking Daffodil heads – Lilies – 'The golden-banded'
one ' – Lily fever – A big Lily.

'Consider the Daffodils'. This was the advice offered by William Robinson to those who wished to enjoy what he called Wild Gardening. It was a style he had invented and to which in 1870 he had devoted a whole book. Struck by the beauty of wild Daffodils in fields in Sussex, he had the idea that similar displays could be enjoyed in the grounds of large houses if owners planted Daffodils of all sorts and other spring bulbs in the grass and under the parkland trees. These areas could be complemented by planting Primroses, Cyclamens, Gentians and Lily-of-the-Valley on mossy banks and by sowing round and about the seeds of 'stout bienni-als' such as Foxglove and Evening Primrose. Robinson considered that such flowers thrived and looked better in rough places than in flower beds in 'stiff' gardens. When it came to creating a wild garden he acknowledged that some people might find it difficult at first to get away from the idea of formal planting in masses, but advised that they look at the natural groupings of wild flowers and, indeed, 'for those who have the means to enjoy this bold and noble phase of gardening – Con-sider the Daffodils'.

Aged barely 14, Harry did not have the financial means of Mr Robinson's meaning, but he did have to consider Daffodils quite hard, in exactly the way Mr Robinson required. It happened on the Monday morning of his first week in his first job. His Uncle Fred had taken him down to the front of the mansion at Blackmoor to meet Lady Selborne and, after introductions, her ladyship announced her intention to have bulbs planted. The chauffeur was called to bring Lady Selborne's electric wheelchair. This was a new form of conveyance and required the chauf-feur to show her how it worked and to oversee a yard or two of progress. With the chair sorted out, Uncle Fred and Harry carried large packages of bulbs to a group of trees on the south side of the moat. Uncle Fred showed his nephew how to open the packages and explained to him that he had to scatter the bulbs on the ground and that where each fell was the spot in which it had to be planted. Uncle Fred then went off to his other duties and Harry was left with Lady Selborne who proceeded to direct operations from her chair. She was, Harry remembers, a very knowledgeable lady when it came to horticulture and had in her mind exactly what was to go where and which bag he should open next. At first it was a bit of a trial for Harry; sometimes he threw them too far and sometimes not far enough, but he soon cottoned on and the job continued for several mornings until all the packages were empty. For many years afterwards Harry went back to Blackmoor in the spring and saw the results of those mornings' work; the blooms of countless Daffodils interspersed with other spring bulbs gave abiding pleasure.

If William Robinson had been far-sighted enough to prophesy the enjoyment afforded by Daffodils planted in a 'natural' style, he was also sufficiently perceptive to appreciate the benefits of purely accidental plantings. In a late edition of *The English Flower Garden* he wrote that, in the period when hardy plants were cast aside in favour of bedding plants, many Daffodils which had been initially thrown out as garden refuse had found their way into orchards and meadows. Robinson noted that it was these chance growths which helped to preserve Daffodils lost to the garden. So it proved, for at the start of Harry's very last job, the one he has held as head gardener since late 1947, the truth of Robinson's words on Daffodils again became apparent.

In the spring of 1948 Harry noticed a great variety of old types of Daffodils growing in a small orchard at Chilton, beyond the north wall of the kitchen garden and across the way from the boiler house and compost heaps. These flowers were something of a mystery for, when questioned, not even the two or three men who had been working at the gardens since before the First World War could remember their planting. Each year these Daffodils appear, though not as freely, it must be admitted, as they did when Harry first saw them, for the small orchard is past its best and any flower which ventures up has to push a breathing space through nettles and briars. The Daffodils are an interesting lot. Some have their petals set so far apart that, as Harry says, you can see daylight right through them, and others have bent-over heads which won't come out fully at all unless they consider conditions favourable.

Among the flower buds showing each early spring Harry recognises the little wild Lenten Daffodil (*N. pseudonarcissus*). This, he says, whatever the weather, is usually in flower by the end of February. In years gone by when there was still a market for such and the mansion had greater call for them, the Lenten Daffodils used to be picked in the bud stage and taken into an 'early' Peach house where there was sufficient heat to get them to open. They used, Harry says, to form a useful part of weekend decorations in the mansion. Although the Lenten Daffodil is

Previous page: A bank of daffodils *by Alfred William Parsons (1847–1920)*

early, many of the other old sorts flowered late, probably a reason for their demise from popularity. When it makes its appearance by a clump of nettles, Harry can put a name to the old Pheasant's Eye (*Narcissus poeticus*). Virgil described this as 'the brightly shining Narcissus' and it is easy to see why for it has snow-white petals surrounding a short crown rimmed with scarlet. *Narcissus poeticus* has a sister flower, the white double *N. poeticus albus plenus odoratus*, though this is not in Harry's collection of old Daffodils and, it seems, sadly not likely ever to be, for 1990 was the last year in which it was listed in the catalogue of one of the remaining bulb companies to carry it. Despite its fragrance no one seems to want white double *poeticus* and so it has become commercially unviable. Other old sorts have also fallen by the wayside because their yield of bulbs is insufficient – today in the bulb business if you plant 1 ton you need to dig up 2 tons to make a profit.

Apart from the Lenten Daffodil and Pheasant's Eye, although he recognised them by sight as they came up each year (and indeed remembered their sort from his Blackmoor days when his uncle used to say, 'They're very old, boy, they were planted before my time'), Harry could not put a name to any of the other old Daffodils. Last spring, however, when the delicate pale heads nodded up as usual and his mind was at the time understandably very much preoccupied with Victorian flowers, he decided to see if unwittingly he had his own collection in these Daffodils. Walking among them, Harry picked ten sorts. He left a different number to mark each clump and gave the same number to the flower picked from it. Each Daffodil with its number was carefully packed up and sent to an acknowledged Daffodil expert with an accompanying note requesting identification. The reply which soon came was disappointing in some respects but gratifying in others. The almost fifty years of anonymity the Daffodils had presented to Harry would for the most part go on, as only a few could be named. One, with yellow petals and a sweet fragrance, was thought to have a connection with *Narcissus odorus*. Another variety was probably 'Bath's Flame', raised in 1914. A third was 'Horsfieldii' which had been raised in 1845 by John Horsfield, a weaver at Prestwick. He had bred it by crossing his best garden flower with a wild Daffodil growing on the banks of a nearby stream. It had in fact first been sold under the name 'Mrs Harrison Weir' but was bought by a collector and bulb salesman called Peter Barr who sold it as 'Horsfieldii'. Of the other seven Daffodils sent no identification could reliably be given but, interestingly, Peter Barr's name came up again as these seven were apparently typical of varieties known to Narcissus experts as *N.* 'Barri' and *N.* 'Backhousei' types. William Backhouse was raising Daffodils around 1835 and Peter Barr collecting and developing them in the

Left: Watering daffodils *by William Henry Margetson (1861–1940)*

Above: Victorian Christmas cards

Right: Peter Barr

Far right: Narcissus poeticus (*'Pheasant's Eye'*)

mid-1850s. When Backhouse died in 1869, Barr acquired his collection.

It was obvious that Barr had been particularly prominent in the world of Victorian Daffodils and no surprise, after some research, to find that he'd been honoured with the name 'the Daffodil King'. He was born in Govan, Scotland, in 1826 and had an early introduction into bulbs through Tulips. His father, a muslin handloom weaver, was a Tulip fancier and grew them in the family's garden. Peter Barr began his career as a seedsman, first in Ireland and then for Richard Smith's nursery in Worcester. In 1852 he joined the firm of Butler & McCulloch, seed and bulb sellers of Covent Garden in London, at an annual salary of £100. He compiled and wrote the firm's catalogues and gradually his salary rose to £400 a year. In 1859 he had obviously saved enough to buy from the Duke of Bedford the lease of 12 King Street, Covent Garden, and in 1862 he left Butler & McCulloch to begin business there. A year later, in order to clarify the name of a quantity of Daffodils he had purchased, he set up a trial ground at Tooting. This was the beginnings of a vast collection of Daffodils which Barr amassed in his attempts to get together every known species and variety. He added to his collection by purchasing breeders' seedlings and he travelled to Spain, Portugal, the Pyrenees and the Maritime Alps in search of wild Daffodils. By his work, and the hybrids born of his collection, Barr succeeded in popularising what had been for years a neglected flower, restricted to a few sorts. In 1901 his most famous Daffodil was shown to the public. Named 'Peter Barr', its size, form and pure white trumpet earned it, among other awards, a Royal Horticultural Society first-class certificate. Despite its catalogue price of £50, several bulbs were quickly sold.

Peter Barr died in London in 1909. On the day of his funeral, 21 September, a national newspaper noted that Daffodils were to be planted over the grave 'to mark the last resting place of Mr Peter Barr, the man who loved flowers and to whom we owe the general cultivation of Daffodils'. If this was done, I hope that they are still there, for if after all these years the old Daffodils in Harry's orchard appear unfailingly, surely a certain spot in Islington Cemetery must be equally bright each spring.

Once Daffodils have bloomed it is good horticultural practice to resist tidying them up by cutting off the leaves. A plant with its leaves left to die down naturally will bloom well the following year. As Harry explained, if in the past he had been presented with a flower bed full of Daffodils and other spring bulbs and the bed needed to be cleared in order to plant a summer display, a week or two after the blooms had gone and while their leaves were still green he had the bulbs lifted and heeled into the walled garden. However, if Daffodils or the like were planted in grass, they could be left to die down without being moved and, particularly if the garden was a wild one, would soon be overtaken and hidden by other plants. Daffodils so placed did, however, need one job done to them and that was the picking-off of their dead blooms so that they put their energy back into the bulb and not into making seed. This would have been a laborious task in Harry's orchard had he not employed an ingeniously simple method, learned as a boy from the Rector of Blackmoor. The Rector had taken him to a hedgerow and cut a stick of hazel out of it. The stick was about 4 feet (1.2 m) long and nicely swishy. He then showed Harry how, by flicking the stick from side to side as he walked, he could take the dead Daffodil heads off as clean as a whistle. From then on, marching up and down through the Rector's Daffodils, the youthful Harry found that dead-heading had turned from a chore into something quite thrilling. Undulled by the years – in fact if anything, quite perfected – Harry's swishing technique soon decapitated the faded Pheasant's Eye blooms and as quickly sped through 'Horsfieldii' and all its unidentified brethren.

If in his lifetime Peter Barr had been assiduous in his pursuit of classifying Daffodils, he was no less keen to be right over Lilies. The Victorian Lily expert Dr A. Wallace, writing of *Lilium speciosum* in his book *Notes on Lilies and their Culture* published in 1879, records 'Sometime since Mr Barr submitted to us a considerable number of specimens of Speciosum, with a view to getting their nomenclature definitely settled.' In fact Barr had in earlier years misnamed *L. speciosum*: in a catalogue he wrote for Butler & McCulloch in 1860 he had called it *Lilium lancifolium*. This was a forgiveable error and he was far from being alone in making it, for it appears that when *L. speciosum* was first introduced it had been wrongly named *L. lancifolium* and that name had stuck. (As an aside, the name *lancifolium* could still be causing confusion, because recently there has been a dictate in the Lily world that *L. tigrinum* – the old orange Tiger Lily – should be called *L. lancifolium*. This is perhaps a pity because, untiger-like though its spotted appearance is – although some think the name refers to the spotted jaguar – the name Tiger Lily has fitted the plant well enough for over a century and a half.)

In 1860 the then *L. lancifolium* (or, to be correct, *L. speciosum*) was referred to in Butler & McCulloch's autumn catalogue as the 'Queen of Lilies' and as being 'unequalled'. Without a view to sales, *L. speciosum* received other, rather odder, accolades. A correspondent writing to a gardening journal of the time felt impelled to impart the following:

When my family are at the seaside, I am in the habit of bringing down tins of flowers, but, owing to the sea air, or gas in the room, or from some other cause, their life is a very short one. Rose and

Above top: Lilium auratum

Above: L. tigrinum (*now* L. lancifolium)

Left: Although this 1850s' watercolour identifies these Lilies as lancifolium *it is believed that they are* Lilium speciosum albiflorum *and* speciosum roseum

Japanese Anemones flag very much after the second day, but *L. speciosum rubrum* brought down a week ago, is still beautiful.

Introduced from Japan in 1832, the beautiful *L. speciosum* held its own as 'Queen of Lilies' until 1862 when the arrival of another Japanese Lily forced it to abdicate. In July of that year Chelsea nurserymen James Veitch & Son exhibited a Lily collected by John Gould Veitch. It was called *Lilium auratum* (the Golden-Banded Lily). Ten thousand people flocked to see this plant which was later reported to have

> taken captive the startled senses of all, not merely horticulturalists, but the public generally, by the enormous size and number of the flowers, their powerful fragrance, their elegant and graceful contour, their richness of ornamentation on a pure white ground and by the general stateliness of the plant.

Demand to obtain *L. auratum* was enormous. Hundreds of thousands of bulbs were shipped from Japan where the Lily grew wild on wooded hillsides. The Japanese called it *Yama Uri* (the Hill Lily). With the passion for *auratum* came a desire to collect and grow other kinds of Lilies. It was an understandable progression, for new Lilies were being introduced not only from Japan but also from America, India and Siberia. Interest in Lilies had outstripped written information on them. One collector, Gloucestershire landowner John Elwes, decided to rectify the situation by publishing his own book, *Elwes' Monograph of the Genus Lilium*. This is particularly magnificent, for Elwes employed as his illustrator the famous nineteenth-century botanical artist William Hood Fitch.

By the mid-1870s Lily collecting had grown to such a pitch that garden journals began to refer to 'Lily Fever'. It was an ailment which could abate quite suddenly, leaving the victim poorer and wiser. Such a case was that of a man who, despite the fact that *L. auratum* at the time of planting cost £6 per dozen bulbs (and some other Lilies were just as pricy), placed in his garden 5000 examples of this species; 1000 *L. speciosum* and 1000 *L. longiflorum* (the latter, like *auratum*, having been introduced in 1862). In addition to these he had beds containing half-dozens and dozens of rarer kinds of Lily. All these added up to the grand total of 10 000 individual bulbs. After six years of fine displays the man noticed a few varieties showing signs of disease: the leaves and stems appeared 'rusty' and there were small black spots on the bulbs. Despite his attempts at remedial action, the disease spread through his entire collection and took with it for good measure common wild species he'd transplanted into his garden from nearby fields. The 'Typhoid Marys' of this particular tragedy were thought to be imported Japanese bulbs

recently added to the collection. Other Lily growers experienced similar disappointments, bulbs of *L. auratum* in particular 'dwindling away and disappearing in the most mysterious manner possible'.

The rotting was attributed to a virulent fungus which was present in the atmosphere and could penetrate the tender skin of a bulb newly lifted from the wild. In an attempt to combat the fungus it was suggested that, as soon as Japanese diggers extracted a bulb from the earth, they should practise the code recently laid down by Professor Lister in his process of 'Antiseptic Surgery' and steep it in one part carbolic to forty parts of water. Whether this was done is not known, but the New Plant & Bulb Company of Colchester did succeed in implementing another method of preservation. They sent instructions to their agents in Japan to get the packers to prepare a large quantity of soft puddled clay and coat each *auratum* bulb in it to the thickness of ¾ inch (2 cm). This coating was then to be wrapped in fine paper which would stop the clay cracking and falling off the bulbs when laid out in the sun to dry. Once dry the clay-coated bulbs were to be packed into boxes and loose soil or sawdust dropped in to fill up the gaps and stop any movement during transportation. This hermetic sealing helped to cut down the large number of rotten bulbs found when packing cases were opened, but ironically the time was approaching when large numbers of bulbs were no longer needed. Lily fever, dosed with failure, began to abate.

In 1903 the discovery of the Regal Lily in a remote valley in Sichuan, China, brought something of a revival of interest, for when sufficient bulbs had been raised from its seed they were found to be easy to cultivate. The tremendous growth in the hybridisation of Lilies which has taken place since the Second World War has also helped reinstate the Lily to popularity. One of the aims of hybridisers is to build in disease resistance, and many of their brightly coloured Lily hybrids now appear in catalogues for amateur gardeners. Despite the ease with which these can be grown and their own particular beauty, there are some Lily purists who still prefer the ethereal loveliness of species such as *L. auratum* and *L. speciosum*. As a footnote, there is another species of Lily which is equally beautiful but in a much larger way, *Cardiocrinum giganteum*. It has shining heart-shaped leaves on a stem which can reach 10 feet (3 m) in height. *Cardiocrinum giganteum* was a popular plant in wild gardens and Harry recalls that when he gardened for the Earl of Bessborough at Stansted it grew in a damp spinney on the estate. The plant does not have a reputation for being difficult, but you do need patience for, according to Harry, a *C. giganteum* grown from seed takes seven years to bloom. When it does it looks magnificent – and so it should because, being monocarpic, it's an event which only happens once.

Left: Cardiocrinum giganteum *growing in* woodland

CHAPTER FIVE
Conservatories and Stovehouses

*Glasshouses – Importing exotic plants – Gardeners and geography –
'Slaughter houses' – Lady Katherine's 'Flowering Corridor' –
The show house – Refurbishing the stovehouse – Vagaries of water systems.*

'Houses of magnificent forms, and almost as light within as in the open day.' This was the vision seen by John Loudon as he wrote about the construction of stovehouses in his *Encyclopaedia of Gardening* (1834). Using wrought-iron bars (a product of the Industrial Revolution), such houses were quite possible to build. Slim but strong, iron bars allowed more light into glasshouses than their wooden counterparts. They could also be cast into huge curves and used to build glasshouses on what was known as the 'curvilinear principle'. These were an extension of the theory that a globe was the most efficient shape for letting in light. Globes, however, not being the most convenient shape to contain conventional plant beds and paths, curvilinear houses were favoured.

Left: A Young Lady in a Conservatory *by Jane Maria Bowkett (1860–85)*

Below: 1885 engraving of a circular span-roof conservatory

The grandeur Loudon foresaw for his curvilinear stovehouse was heightened by the fact that the Palms it might contain would not become etiolated through being too far away from the roof glass. This being the case the roof could soar to 150 feet (45 m) from the ground and 'admit of the tallest Oriental trees and the undisturbed flight of birds among the branches'. Loudon considered that this roof, owing to its lightweight nature, could cover several acres and the hollow cast-iron columns helping to support it could usefully double as downpipes for rainwater.

Glasshouses of magnificent form (albeit not 150 feet high) did become a reality. In 1840 Joseph Paxton, head gardener at Chatsworth House in Derbyshire, had built for the Sixth Duke of Devonshire a structure known as the Grand Conservatory. Paxton employed the curvilinear principle but in fact used wood for the bars, not iron. He helped the ingress of light into the conservatory by having the glass panes set in a manner known as ridge and furrow. Because of its upright and sloping shape this method of glazing caught sunlight whatever the position of the sun in the sky. The entrances to the conservatory were so wide that when Queen Victoria went to see it in 1843 her carriage could drive straight in. A garden journalist visiting Chatsworth thirty years after its erection described the Grand Conservatory as 'a magnificent structure covering an acre [0.5 hectare] of ground, it is 277 feet [84.5 m] long by 123 feet [37.5 m] wide and the central transept is 67 feet [20.5 m] high with a span of 70 feet [21.3 m].' For reasons of economy it was demolished in 1920. However, another monster glasshouse of the era still stands, its magnificence retained by the help of an £8 million renovation programme completed in 1988. It is the Palm House at the Royal Botanic Gardens at Kew in London. Built between 1844 and 1848, this huge curvilinear house is ribbed by sixty wrought-iron half-arches. Interestingly it has a number of cast-iron support pillars designed to carry, as Loudon had suggested that such might, rainwater from the roof.

Joseph Paxton was responsible for perhaps the grandest glasshouse of all time. It was built for the Great Exhibition of 1851. *Punch* dubbed it the Crystal Palace. It was three times the length of St Paul's Cathedral and high enough to enclose some of the tallest trees within Hyde Park. This extraordinary glass structure was eventually removed from Hyde Park to Sydenham. Sir Joseph Paxton, who was knighted in 1851, had a house on the summit of Sydenham Hill, in fact no more (in the rather unfortunate phrase of Donald Beaton, editor of the *Cottage Gardener and Country Gentleman*) 'than a stone's throw' from the Crystal Palace. Such missiles withstanding, the palace stood until it was destroyed by fire in 1936.

A tropical plant stove heated by water pipes

In addition to the use of cast iron, several other factors helped the rise of the Victorian glasshouse. One was an improvement in the manufacture of sheet glass and another an innovation in heating methods. In the 1830s boilers began to be used to pump hot water through a series of flow-and-return pipes. This method of heating was particularly suitable for establishments which had ranges of glasshouses or single large structures (the Great Conservatory at Chatsworth had 6 miles (9.5 km) of hot-water pipes), but for gardens with only one glasshouse the old way of heating by hot air in flues persisted for many years. In fact Harry remembers that his first introduction to a flued house was when he started work for the Rector of Blackmoor in 1934. The Rectory garden had a lean-to glasshouse with a small stoke hole and a big fire box built into one end. Hot air from the fire travelled along a flue laid down on the ground and exited at the opposite end.

Despite its efficiency the method of heating by hot-water pipes had a drawback; whereas the plants imported from hot, dry regions did well in the hot, dry atmosphere created by flue heat, they failed in the kind of heat that pipes gave.

Hot-water pipes might have caused the demise of certain plants but they had others to warm – in fact a great many. Increasingly vast

Left: The Tropical House at the Royal Botanic Gardens, Kew. Painting by Thomas Greenhalgh

Right: The Victorian conservatory like the drawing room was a place for 'frequent resort and agreeable assemblage at all seasons'

numbers were being sent to Britain by plant hunters collecting for botanic gardens, large nurseries or private individuals. The hunting grounds were the temperate parts of America, Australasia, India, South Africa, Japan and China. The healthy arrival in Britain of these new discoveries was dependent upon the means of their dispatch from their place of origin. This could be effected in a number of ways. One ingenious method, useful in that the materials were often to hand, was to split in half a piece of bamboo stem. Cuttings from a newly discovered plant were then inserted between the two halves and they were tied back together with bark or twine. Once both ends were plugged with clay, this impregnated baton could be sewn up in stout wax cloth and addressed with its destination. Other methods included the use of India sheet rubber to make bundles of cuttings airtight and watertight before plunging them into ships' water tanks or into their ice rooms. A method which was found particularly satisfactory (it was responsible for the introduction from the Himalayas to Europe of the *Cardiocrinum giganteum*) was wrapping cuttings or bulbs in wax cloth and giving the cloth numerous coats of liquid soap and wax.

For seeds and plants the greatest aid to safe conveyance was a wooden box with glazed sides and top. These were known as Wardian cases after their inventor Nathaniel B. Ward. An interesting account referring to their use appeared in the *Quarterly Review* of 1842:

> There are few ships that now arrive from the East Indies without carrying on deck several cases of this description, belonging to one or other of our chief nurserymen, filled with orchideous plants and other new and tender varieties from the East, which formerly baffled the utmost care to land them here in a healthy state. These cases, frequently furnished by the extreme liberality of Dr Wallich the enterprising and scientific director of the Hon. Company's gardens in the neighbourhood of Calcutta, form on shipboard a source of great interest to the passengers of a four-month's voyage, and, after having deposited their precious contents on the shores, return again by the same ships filled with the common flowers of England. . . . This interchange of sweets was a few years ago almost unattainable, the sea-air and spray, as is well known, being most injurious to every kind of plant; but their evil effects are now completely avoided by these air-tight cases, which admit no exterior influence but the light.

The success of Wardian cases lay in the fact that, given a basis of good soil and watered well before sealing down, plants placed in them could exist for months without any further attention. Self-sufficiency was achieved by the occupant taking up water through its roots and evaporating it through its leaves, and the subsequent condensation running down the inside of the glass re-wetting the soil. Ward had discovered this principle by accident. He had filled, as a home for a moth chrysalis, a large bottle with moist leaf mould, sealed it and put it into the open air. To his surprise a fern and a grass sprang up in the bottle and both plants lived for three years without watering or the lid being removed. Rain accidentally getting into the bottle eventually destroyed the plants. No contemporary account of this minor miracle mentions what happened to the moth. When Nathaniel Ward died in 1869, reference was made in an obituary notice to the 'valuable plants' his cases had transported. Not the least of these were tea seeds and plants from China to India. Plant collector Robert Fortune, knowing that tea seeds quickly lost their viability, planted them into soil in Wardian cases. Fortune employed the same method to introduce tea plants safely into America, but tea growing did not become a major industry there as it did in India.

Despite reading in their threepenny weeklies such sprightly introductions as 'Rejoice my brother gardeners and all amateur lovers and growers of plants for this gem is likely soon to be seen in our collections . . .', head gardeners must have furrowed their brows more than once when called on to grow perfectly plants which were foreign to them in every sense. It is small wonder that the same weeklies espoused the need for gardeners to master geography in order to understand the distribution of plants. Such an understanding was useful to Mr Doug Holt whom I have the privilege to know. Doug is now eighty-nine. He started working life as a garden boy and went on to become a nurseryman. One of his first jobs was to work at Shawford Park, Twyford, Hampshire. Frank Kingdon-Ward, a man often referred to as the last of the great plant collectors, used to send finds to Shawford, and Doug, after reading the accompanying labels which had the place of origin and altitude found written on them, had to decide what treatment was needed. In the case of *Meconopsis baileyi*, the Blue Poppy Kingdon-Ward discovered on an expedition to Tibet in 1924, Doug decided, quite correctly, that coolness was the best policy for several weeks. Kingdon-Ward also brought Lilies to Shawford. When they flowered they were exhibited at Chelsea and won a medal. Other introductions raised in the garden were not so successful. A Primula called 'Tyrolean Red' was, Doug says, not worth looking at, and an Iris named after the garden owner's wife also had an ignoble end – the owner not thinking much of it, the Iris got left behind when the family moved.

Even with geography sorted out and their plants growing in a healthy state, some Victorian gardeners found that their efforts were confounded by what they called 'slaughter houses'. These were certain sorts of conservatories which, particularly after the tax on glass was lifted in 1845, sprang up against villas and mansions. Slaughter houses were designed by architects to complement the design of the house to which they were attached. Sometimes these lofty edifices completed one wing of a mansion and accordingly were built of heavy stone, iron and rolled glass. Their darkness, poor ventilation and fluctuating temperature (for it was often difficult to keep frost out without making the atmosphere too dry) earned these structures their sombre soubriquet. Once admitted between their stone pilasters, healthy pot plants went into terminal decline. These victims had been raised to the point of flowering in the more congenial greenhouses and pits of the kitchen garden. Their conveyance to the conservatory was to provide, as all conservatories were supposed to do, 'enjoyment and display' for the owners of the house.

Shirley Hibberd, in his *The Amateur's Greenhouse and Conservatory* (1888), defined a conservatory as being related to the drawing room 'and adapted for frequent resort and agreeable assemblage at all seasons, and especially at times of festivity'. Its social value was such that, for those party-givers without one, temporary conservatories could be built and fixed – a particular speciality of the Pine Apple Nursery, Maida Vale, London.

In early Victorian days it was the practice for gardeners to fill conservatories with solid banks of flowering plants, not only for effect but to disguise the surface of the benches, or staging, on which the pots stood. As time went by this began to attract criticism for, despite the number of plants used and the work entailed, visitors gave such displays only passing notice. More tasteful and eye-catching arrangements were sought. One method recommended in the 1880s was to do away with side staging altogether and put in its place 'rock-bed arrangements'. Pots of large flowering plants could be sunk into these and their smaller counterparts camouflaged by Ferns and Selaginellas which had been planted in a band of earth. The back bed could be given over to widely spaced Camellias and Orange trees interspersed with tall Palms, and could at the same time provide a good position for climbing plants. This design was particularly suited to those individuals with large conservatories but little income.

Such persons not being the owners of any of the establishments in which Harry worked, he is perfectly conversant with the old and costly method of staging flowering plants. In fact Lady Katherine Ashburnham of Ashburnham Place near Battle, East Sussex, had *two* conservatories to keep up. One was the grand orthodox kind and built onto the west end of the mansion. It was very elaborate, Harry recalls, filled with Palms and

How to carry a handbarrow single-handed

batches of plants that had been grown in the walled kitchen garden. These were carried up from the garden on a handbarrow, something like a bier, an example of which is still in use in Harry's present garden. It doesn't have wheels, a useful asset when negotiating glasshouse steps, but relies on two pairs of gardeners' legs: one pair beneath the handles at either end to carry it along. The handbarrow was also used to transport enormous old Cactus plants which flowered each spring. When not taken to the conservatory, the Cacti lived in a glasshouse attached to the second, less orthodox conservatory at Ashburnham, a 40-foot (12-m)-long structure known as 'the Flowering Corridor'.

'The Corridor' was in the walled kitchen garden. On her visits to see it Lady Katherine left the mansion and traversed a route known as 'The Long Walk'. By this approach she did not have to enter through the frame yard and glass department but could come straight to a door which opened into the little walled garden where the Flowering Corridor was situated. The lengthy lean-to stretched along a wall and inside it, trained against the wall and up to the roof, were Geraniums, both ivy-leaved and otherwise, and alternately, *Asparagus sprengeri* and *A. plumosus* 'ferns'. The height of this wall, Harry remembers, was the equivalent of that of the back wall in his peach house at Chilton. As this is roughly 15 feet (4.5 m), Geraniums trained to roof height must have looked quite something, particularly as, the house being heated, they flowered the year round. There were lengths of staging in the Corridor and in the middle part tiers which, according to Harry, were always staged up summer and winter with flowering plants. He recalls that, during his short stay at Ashburnham, on at least three or four occasions when the Flowering Corridor was staged up, to his knowledge the only people to see and appreciate it were the gardeners. Nevertheless as each display passed over it was replaced.

Once flowers left the walled garden for the conservatory attached to the mansion they became the responsibility of the pleasure-ground gardeners. However, the staging of flowers in the Flowering Corridor, it being within the walled garden complex, was carried out by the inside foreman and by Harry in his capacity as journeyman. It was also their task every Friday afternoon to go through the Corridor until, by five o'clock, there wasn't a weed in a pot or a dead leaf or dead flower to be seen. They worked with small hand brushes and round skip baskets. As each progressed he used his foot to push the basket along the floor. The floor itself was cleaned by the lad under Harry and the foreman. On Saturday mornings this lad scrubbed the red quarry tiles so well that, Harry says, when he'd finished you could have eaten your meals off it. Harry was a good judge of this degree of cleanliness. As a young journeyman at

Stansted Park he had been allotted a similar task: to wash the floor of a glass porch set into the centre of a fruit range. The porch was always staged up with pot plants. On Sunday mornings washing had to be extra thorough, for the family visited the gardens after attending church.

Although the mansion on Harry's present estate is porticoed and pillared, its Victorian owners, thankfully, never felt the need to build a 'slaughter house' conservatory against it. Instead, they preferred to see flowers displayed in a sensible span-roofed glasshouse. This is situated in the smaller of the estate's two walled kitchen gardens. It runs north to south and, in so doing, stands out from the centre of a range of growing houses which run west to east along the top half of the garden. Despite its conventional glasshouse shape, 'the show house' (as Harry has always known it) has an air of grandeur. The door at the south-facing end is approached by two wide steps, and anyone entering from the north-facing end has to negotiate double doors and two steps down. The house's side and central staging is supported by elegant wrought-iron legs and the pathway dividing them is paved with red tiles set obliquely to form a diamond pattern. As to its overall size the show house amply fulfils the Victorian requirement that there be room enough to allow 'the free movement of full-grown persons attired in a manner which would render it inconvenient for them to come in contact with damp flower-pots'.

However, no elegantly attired people had come to view the contents of flower pots in the showhouse for some years. Owing to this and because it was a sensible shape for his purposes, Harry had for some time been helping his nursery business by using the show house as a greenhouse. The difference between a greenhouse and a conservatory (or, perhaps, show house), according to one Victorian tome, is the same as the difference between luncheon and dinner. Given the opportunity of demonstrating the skills that gardeners 'under glass' used to need, Harry was only too delighted (and indeed the floor turned out to be spotless enough to serve it) to make the show house 'dinner' once again.

The re-glorification of the show house necessitated the metamorphosis of another structure: the stovehouse which was at a right-angle to it. A stove plant, provided that it had been suitably hardened off in an intermediate house, could make a temporary transition between stovehouse and conservatory and supply the latter with exotic colour, especially useful in winter months. The stovehouse in Harry's garden, grown unstove-like over the years, had at first become a house for carnations, then, like the show house, it proved a useful place for Harry's nursery plants. Thomas Baines, who wrote *Greenhouse & Stove Plants*, an edifying book which includes 'Full Details of the Propagation and Cultivation of 500 FAMILIES OF PLANTS, Embracing all the Best Kinds in Cultivation, Suitable for Growing in the Greenhouse, Intermediate House, and Stove', believed that the best stovehouses were those with a span roof. Harry's was span-roofed. The best size apparently was 18 feet (5.5 m wide) and 45–50 feet (14–15.2 m) long; Harry's was 15 feet (4.5 m) wide and 45 feet (14 m) long. Mr Baines further believed that the side stages in stovehouses should all be similar in width, materials and construction and the paths the same; in Harry's they were. As to other internal arrangements Mr Baines was of the opinion that there should be not a central stage, but a brick-built pit, 3 feet (1 m) in depth; Harry's house had this attribute, but would Mr Baines have approved of the black plastic sheeting which covered it? Indeed, it was difficult to see that there was a cavity beneath the plastic, because Harry had fitted it so well. This plastic provided in Harry's eyes an extremely useful surface. It stopped pots placed on it drying out too quickly after being watered. But having entered into the spirit of returning the stovehouse to the way it would have looked in its heyday, Harry sportingly removed the plastic. He went further than that; with the help of young David he wire-brushed all the cast iron grating which the plastic had been covering. It was, he said, the first time it had seen the light of day for twenty-five years.

When the grating was being lifted and brushed, it was possible to see that around the sides at the bottom of the pit was a double row of cast-iron hot-water pipes. There were also supports projecting just above them. Harry recalled that in winter the grating could be lowered on to these and so bring plants placed on it much closer to the heat from the pipes. In summer it could be lifted up to its top position again. In some stovehouses the heat from the pipes was heightened by filling the space between them and the grating with tanner's bark or other fermenting material. In fact this was one point in which Harry's exemplary stovehouse wouldn't have quite met with Mr Baines's approbation. That aficionado couldn't see the use of having pipes at all and believed that a tan bed alone was sufficient. The grating over the pit was in sections, rather like the bases of a number of iron bedsteads. This arrangement later proved a boon to Harry when he found that certain tropical plants were too tall to fit well into the house. By simply removing a grating altogether he could gain a couple of feet of extra height.

The whole of the stovehouse was washed and scrubbed and every gap that was found sealed up. Cool outside air was to enter by invitation only. Heat was a precious commodity. On the subject of heat, it is probably the time to come clean and admit that the embrace given by the iron water pipes wrapped around the interior of Harry's glasshouses was –

quite cold. The agent once responsible for filling them with hot water was a huge round-backed boiler. It still existed, squatting 15 feet (4.5 m) below ground level, a depth needed to help gravity feed. This boiler was, however, as dead as on the day its last ember went out almost thirty years previously. Economy had dictated on that day that it shouldn't be re-lit. Present-day economy, if anything more stringent, echoed that dictate and it was decided to heat the glasshouses with electric blow heaters. They worked on the principle that every time the temperature dropped below a certain level they would spring into life and bring it back up again. Harry had a similar heating system in a large modern greenhouse he used for his nursery business.

At first, despite the ease of use, he found hot-air heating unsatisfactory. It was difficult to explain why, because the temperature of the house was about right, but the loss in heat occasioned every time the blowers went off and maintained until the air was cool enough to bring them back on again seemed to make damp marks and spots on the plants. According to Harry, this was something you never saw in old private gardens where perfection was everything, and you could get perfection from hot-water-pipe heating if you knew how. For example, in summer you usually threw some ashes on to the fire in the boiler as soon as heat wasn't required, then you went through the glasshouses and turned the flow valves off. When the houses were shut up and the temperature began to drop in the evening, you drew up the fire in the boiler and turned the valves back on. You had only an hour or two to get the pipes to the right heat and that was where, he says, experience came in. Harry gained his boiler wisdom by trial and error. When a house was full of plants in flower or fruit just beginning to ripen, the head gardener used to stipulate that by morning he wanted just sufficient heat in the pipes to keep the air dry. He meant what he said, for Harry recalls that on his morning rounds he studied the greenhouse thermometer to see if it was reading between 60 and 65°F (15.5–18°C). Harry learned that this figure couldn't be achieved by being clever and fuelling the boiler too early the evening before because by next morning the house was cold. Slipping out in the evening and coming back to the gardens to stoke the boiler up late didn't work either – in the morning the pipes were too hot. In winter it was the opposite story. Harry had to keep the temperature well *up*. The last stoking of the boiler took place between nine and ten o'clock at night. At Stansted the head gardener, Mr Tomalin, would make his rounds at about 9 pm. Sometimes this coincided with the young duty gardener doing his rounds. However, if the gardener had gone back to the bothy (the house in which under gardeners lodged) and Mr Tomalin found something wrong, he would make him come out

Left: Harry watering show house plants

again. For instance, heat 2°F (1°C) too low was, Harry says, 'lots of trouble' and you weren't allowed to go to bed until the temperature in all the various glasshouses was just right.

The two boilers at Stansted were fuelled by coke or anthracite. Burnt coke used to run into an almost solid mass of clinker. When one boiler was allowed to go out while the other took its place, this clinker had to be completely cleaned out with a long iron scraper. The ash-pit, full of ash and bits of clinker the size of hazelnuts which had dropped from the big pieces, had to be raked out every day. What it yielded was kept in a pile separate from the big pieces. On Friday mornings it was a two-man task to lift the piles of clinker and ash out of the stoke hole. The method was the same in most gardens. A door at the side of the boiler house opened on to a sheer drop. Above the door, fixed to the ceiling, was a pulley wheel furnished with a rope with knots in it. A man standing in the doorway fixed a bucket to the end of the rope and lowered it to his companion standing on the floor 15 feet (4.5 m) below. The man below filled the bucket and shouted for it to be hauled up. The ashes were taken away by wheelbarrow and piled in a secluded spot at the back of the gardens. They weren't rubbish for they would come into their own again to form plunge beds for forcing bulbs.

The boilers at Ashburnham had been easier to keep clean. They were fuelled by wood, four barrow-loads at a time. Unlike clinker, once it was burnt this fell straight into ash. The wood came from the estate and used to arrive at the garden in 4-foot (1.2-m) lengths, described locally as 'bock wood'. Harry had always known its 3-foot (1-m) equivalent in Hampshire as 'cord wood'.

Bock or cord; clinker hoisting, valve turning, stoking-up by lantern light – it all made electric heaters seem rather mundane.

CHAPTER SIX

Plants under Glass

Plant stories – A Fuchsia chandelier – Tying Schizanthus –
Smells and rashes – Foliage plants – Glasshouse tools – David makes a roller
blind – Pot-tapping – The art of 'airing' – Pest control –
Insect-eating plants.

The plants which filled the stovehouse and the show house brought a bit of romance and drama back to proceedings. Take the Daturas, for instance. As Harry says, they are lovely plants with big leaves and large trumpet-like flowers. He remembers tubs brought into flower in August and placed on the mansion terrace at Blackmoor. However, he also has a less pleasant memory of Daturas: he's sure that he once read in an old book that in their country of origin (which wicked country we can't be sure, but if it was sweet-scented *Datura suaveolens* it must have been Mexico) Daturas used to be grown in a circle, and if womenfolk disobeyed their masters they were pegged down overnight in the circle and the heavy scent from the plants was the death of them. There was a certain macabreness about the pots of Amaryllis too. *Flowers From Many Lands*, published by the Religious Tract Society, told readers the alarming tale that 'A juice is obtained from the bulbs and blossom, into which the Hottentots dip the points of their spears, in order to render them fatally venomous.' Then there was *Solanum jasminoides*, a prolifically flowering plant introduced from South America in 1838, but it did so resemble Deadly Nightshade. So much for drama.

Romance presented itself in the incredibly beautiful waxy bells of a Lapageria brought for the stovehouse. Nicholson's *Dictionary* calls Lapageria 'the most beautiful climbing plant in existence.' Originating from Chile, it is named after Josephine Lapagerie (the maiden name of the Empress of France). The Empress was a great plant lover and created a very fine garden at Malmaison. In fact her love of flowers introduced a note of chivalry to the Napoleonic Wars. The English Admiralty ordered that any seeds or plants found on captured enemy vessels and addressed to her should be forwarded with all speed.

In addition to Lapageria there were several pots of another beautiful climber for the stovehouse – Bougainvillea. The splendour of this plant

Datura

is not in the colour of its flowers, which are insignificant, but in the bracts, which on some plants are pale pink and on others a much deeper shade. Bougainvillea, like Lapageria, had romantic if not dramatic connections. It had been named after a Frenchman called Louis Antoine de Bougainville. Bougainville set sail for the South Seas, hoping to find new territories for the French to colonise. He was accompanied by a botanist called Philibert de Commerson, who in turn had a young man assistant. Commerson collected 'Bougainvillea' in Rio de Janeiro. As their journey progressed his assistant helped him with other plant finds, but one day in Tahiti the young man was seized by a native and in the struggle to get him back safely it was discovered that 'he' was in fact a she. This was something of a shock to everyone except Commerson. But it was all quite moral: Mlle Jeanne Baret had persuaded the botanist to take her along for the thrill of the voyage.

Harry was pleased to have pots of Bougainvillea back in the garden. When he first arrived as head gardener in 1947, there were two large pots of it trained up to the gable ends of the show house. The lady of the house told him that they were over fifty years old. One eventually died of old age and the other, because it was too big to move, died when the boiler was turned off for the last time.

Harry put other climbers besides Lapageria and Bougainvillea into the stovehouse and the show house. They might not have had such an interesting past but they were beautiful and did the job they had been employed to do in Victorian times – that is, 'disguise pillars and girders and relieve stiffness and formality'. There was Plumbago, not only blue, but a red one and a white one too. There were also

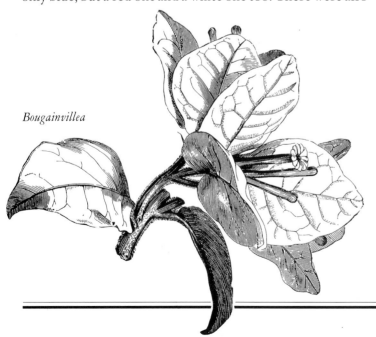

Bougainvillea

Left: An illustration of North American flora taken from Flowers From Many Lands *published* c. 1875

Below: Chinese and Japanese plants from the same book

Right: An 1859 illustration of Lapageria rosea. *It is shown with the shrub* Weigela rosea

Passion Flower plants which grew with incredible speed and produced flowers strangely reminiscent of eyes fringed with lashes, each lasting just a day, closing forever at night. Equally as brief – in fact they could crumple by afternoon – were the startlingly blue flowers of the Morning Glory. This Convolvulus wound itself round a pillar in the show house. Stephanotis flowers, waxy and fragrant, *could* have had their dark leaves trained along girders, but Harry preferred to wind each round hazel sticks bent into an arch across its pot. The Allamandas would have climbed too, given time, but Harry had grown them from cuttings and the plants made only a few feet. They bore magnificent trumpet-shaped yellow blooms. A climber attractive not for its flower but for its ability to be trailed or draped was Smilax. Victorians found that its fresh green colour contrasted well with white tablecloths. Harry grew it in pots just inside the stovehouse door. He didn't try to copy an interesting nine-teenth-century flamboyance – a Fuchsia chandelier. This was something which could have been viewed at Chiswick House, London, in 1874. It adorned the conservatory roof and was created by training a standard Fuchsia against one of the roof supports in the shape of an umbrella. Despite the plant's sap having to negotiate a right-angled bend to get to the 'chandelier', it was, according to *The Garden*'s correspondent, 'a pretty and interesting object, flowering as freely as the branches do that are growing more naturally'.

One of the tallest pot plants put in the show house was the Abutilon. There were two sorts. One had delicately veined primrose-yellow

Above left: Passion Flower
Below: The Fuchsia chandelier

flowers, the other rusty-red ones. To the uninitiated it looked as if their petals might open wide, but they remained rounded like frail down-turned egg cups. Smaller in stature were pots of Tibouchina. Sometimes known as Brazilian Spider Plants, many of these were introduced in Victorian times. They have grey-green downy leaves and rich purple flowers about 1 inch (2.5 cm) in diameter.

In spring, after the forced bulbs (see Chapter Eight), a large part of the staging in the show house was given over to Cinerarias and Schizanthus. The tall Schizanthus, with their butterfly blooms, looked showy but their appearance came at a cost. Before they bloomed each one was given a single central thin stick and all the shoots tied to it. They were tied in the place the shoot was growing naturally. This, Harry said, was to avoid the plant ending up looking like a birch broom. In the old days a job given to a young journeyman, it involved taking a piece of bass (raffia) and splitting it very thin. This was twisted once round the central cane and then twisted over and over on itself until it was the thickness of a strand of cotton, when it was ready to tie in the shoot with a reef-knot. It was a technique known as May-pole tying. The task took hours and it needed doing three or four times before the Schizanthus flowered. It had to be done to stop the plant branching out too much because, having no solidity to the stem, it would topple over, but the tying-in had to be unnoticeable. These old tall Schizanthus helped to fill what Harry called an important gap from round about Easter until the middle of June. Despite the work they take he still believes they're better than the modern 12-inch (30-cm) sort.

Pots of Arum Lilies and a large tub of Clivia, with its dark leaves and deep orange flowers, also helped to brighten the show house in the spring months. Clivia (named after the Duchess of Northumberland, a member of the Clive family) had been discovered by the plant hunter James Bowie in South Africa in 1823. A year later Bowie found the ancestor of the pots of Streptocarpus which bloomed in the stovehouse in summer. The plant, also known as the Cape Primrose, was discovered on the land of an illegitimate son of George III who had been discreetly sent to the Cape Colony. The man called himself, less discreetly, George Rex and the plant became *Streptocarpus rex*. Perhaps tactlessly, on the side staging of the stovehouse opposite to Streptocarpus was a magnificent *Strelitzia reginae*. It had been named in honour of George III's wife, Charlotte of Mecklenburg-Strelitz, and was found in South Africa by collector Francis Masson in 1773. It is better known as Bird-of-Paradise Flower and it's easy to see why. A beak-like protuberance points out at right angles at the top of a tall stem. The 'beak' is surmounted by a crest of blue-and-orange petals.

Strelitzia reginae

Above: An Abutilon gives height to a display in the show house

Left: An Orchid in the show house backed by tall Schizanthus

Right: The show house in spring

Below: Cockscombs

On the subject of birds, it was also easy to see why *Celosia cristata* is known as Cockscomb. Harry grew these oddities from seed to decorate the show house. The horizontal span of velvety flowers looks as though it has been compressed until it undulates like a cock's comb. In 1878 Messrs Carters, seed merchants, succeeded in growing this plant with a rich crimson comb 3 feet 2 inches (96 cm) in length. At its thickest part the comb was 1 foot 4 inches (40.5 cm) across. This giant was described as 'highly ornamental' and was called the Empress Cockscomb.

The show house displayed less exotic plants which, as the year progressed, proved their worth in their ability to keep in flower. One was *Cuphea ignea*, which Harry called the cigar plant: its small red cylindrical blooms are tipped with a ring of light grey, like the ash on a burning cigar. Fuchsias and Pelargoniums seemed always to provide colour. So for a long spell did the pendulate purplish-red Love-Lies-Bleeding, living up to its botanical name *Amaranthus* ('a' meaning 'not' and 'maraino' meaning 'wither'). A South American plant with compact yellow and orange rosettes called Lantana also bloomed unceasingly. It belied its description in Shirley Hibberd's *The Amateur's Greenhouse and Conservatory*. He had called it 'comparatively useless' and wrote that the odour of the foliage was so unpleasant that it was useless for making a bouquet. Perhaps over the years it has improved, because no one found the smell offensive. The palm for offending most people in that direction went to a Cape bulb called Eucomis. It became part of the stovehouse restoration project by virtue of having been kindly donated by programme presenter and adviser Peter Thoday, and it reached Harry's garden via a short stay in a BBC office. The stay was short because complaints were many. The Eucomis flower spike gave off a powerful, strange smell. In its proper place in the stovehouse this smell wasn't evident; perhaps it was tempered by space and the sweet scent of Orange blossom and Jasmine. This tale isn't intended to malign the Eucomis for, with its brown-spotted stem, it is a very handsome plant.

There was one particular flowering plant which never made an appearance among the collection Harry produced to keep the show house decorated. It was *Primula obconica*. This had been introduced to Britain from central China in 1882 and Harry had been introduced to it sometime in the mid-1930s, when he was working for Captain Thackeray of Wode House at Headley. The Captain had *Primula obconica* in flower constantly in the long entrance corridor leading to his front door. They were planted on staging on wire mesh covered with moss three or four times a year. It was Harry's task to tend these Primulas but he found that the leaves brought him out in a rash. At night the blisters on his hands and arms itched, so he scratched them, but this made the irritation spread to such an extent that he was forced to go to a doctor. He was told that he must not work with *Primula obconica* again. However, when he took up his last job his new employers professed a liking for the plant and so he manfully tried once more. It proved to be a rash move. Lady Ward saw and understood the problem and the Primulas haven't been in the garden since, nor will be.

Flowering plants, beautiful as their appearance was, were not the only attractions in the stovehouse. Rising above them we had Palms: essential residents for, if *The Garden* of June 1874 was to be believed, grouped with other plants they added dignity and relieved monotony. The risk of monotony seemed to trouble many Victorian writers on stovehouse culture. There was a general concensus of opinion that to avoid it, it was wise to keep plants potted, and thus mobile, than unpotted and rooted to one spot. We had a wide enough range of sorts (by kind temporary donation) to avoid monotony even in the Palms themselves. There were full-fronded ones which looked like Coconut trees but without the tall trunk; others with fan-shaped leaves; and, more delicate and easier to manoeuvre than their colleagues, slender Oil Palms. Harry rendered them all dignified but not overpowering in height by removing the grating at various intervals and placing their pots low down inside the central pit. A Bird's-nest Fern proved too big even for this treatment and in the summer months had to be dispatched to stand in the show house. It turned out to be a happy move, for the top steps at the south-facing end of the show house provided a vantage point from which to look down into it and see the insides of its leaves which were a surprising tan colour.

Banana plants, provided that they were given enough space to spread their huge tender leaves, sat happily on top of the pit grating in the stovehouse. When the sun shone through them, these leaves turned a bright translucent green. In the early morning its rays also transformed the spiky foliage of two Dracaenas, brightening them from dark maroon to a vibrant plum colour. Although I cannot be sure of their variety, it is quite likely that these Dracaenas originated from among the many richly coloured kinds introduced into Britain by John Gould Veitch. The grandson of James Veitch who had set up the family nursery business in the late years of the eighteenth century, John was the first member of the family to travel abroad to collect plants. In Australia and the South Sea Islands he found and brought back home not only Dracaenas but also other stove plants, including brilliant-leaved Crotons. The popularity of these plants and their number rose to such an extent that when William Hugh Gower of the Nurseries, Tooting, in London, was asked to make a selection of Crotons for Cassell's *Popular Gardening* (circa 1880), he listed almost fifty and admitted that it was a difficult job to limit himself to that number. Mr Gower believed them to be indispensable in the plant stovehouse and thought that their brilliance and the diversity of their markings rendered them 'quite as showy as flowers'.

The idea of foliage holding its own among flowers had been given impetus by various publications. In 1870 a firm of publishers asked Shirley Hibberd to write the text to accompany an illustrated work to be called *New and Rare Beautiful-Leaved Plants*. In the preface of the book he states:

> The increased attention paid to Beautiful-leaved Plants constitutes a distinct phase in the history of horticulture. It is but recently that the beauty of leaves has been fully recognised, and the passion that has arisen for collecting and cultivating 'fine-foliaged plants', is one of the newest, but is not at all likely to be transient.

The book was published in monthly parts at 1 shilling (5p) each; the illustrations are stunning and a bound complete volume today must be very valuable. An equally finely illustrated book, *Beautiful Leaved Plants*, held its popularity. It was originally published in 1861 but in 1891 a third edition was issued. Its authors, E. J. Lowe and W. Howard, saw the book as a guide from which those with limited growing space could make a choice. It was as suitable for those with no space to grow the plants at all, for they could 'have a copy of them on the drawing-room table'.

Surely no one would have been content with a picture alone if they could have had the real plant of *Alocasia metallica*. Discovered in Borneo in 1860, this plant was variously described as like a chameleon, changing its colour according to the angle from which it was viewed, or suggesting to 'the spectator that he is looking at some elaborate work of metallic art'. Sadly, it didn't grace Harry's stovehouse. One was tracked down at a nursery in Hampshire but it had to stay there because it would have cost £60 to buy it.

Harry did have plenty of another beautiful-leaved Victorian favourite – the Coleus. This was sometimes known as 'the cottager's Croton', because on sunny cottage windowsills it developed brilliant colours. He also had a Coleus oddity, *C. thyrsoideus*, whose attraction lay not in its leaves (which closely resembled those of an ordinary nettle) but in its blue flowers. It had apparently become rare through being sticky and unmarketable.

Prized in nineteenth-century stovehouses for their colour rather than their fine leaves were Caladiums and Begonias. Particularly favoured was *Begonia rex*. Every so often Harry augmented his supply of this by seeking out on existing plants what he called 'middle-grade' leaves – ones which were neither too young nor too old. If he found a suitable example, Harry picked it, turned it over and laid it flat on a bench, then with his penknife made several slanting cuts, each about 1½ inches (4 cm) long, across the ribs exposed on the leaf's underside. Each leaf was then laid (right way up) flat on to a pan of prepared sandy compost. A few walnut-sized stones laid on it stopped the leaf from curling up away from the compost. It was then watered and covered over with a bell glass. Very soon the cuts callused over and little nobbles, each something like a Sweet Pea seed, formed. It was from these that the tiny new

Illustrations from New and Rare Beautiful-Leaved Plants, *1870*

Begonias sprouted until they were big enough to be cut off and potted into 2½-inch (6-cm) pots. In quick growing seasons, Harry says, a leaf will give a second crop if put back on to the compost.

The bell glasses which cocooned the above propagation looked old but were not. They had been made for Harry by a glassblower called Neil Wilkin. He had worked to an 1880s' design and fortunately had an oven large enough to take the glasses once they were blown. Unlike many which were formerly used on outside borders, the design for this bell glass incorporated a 'super glass'. This was a detachable top which looked like an inverted wine glass with a knob instead of a stem. The super glass sealed an opening in the crown of the bell glass and by moving it you could adjust the temperature in the glass. It also served, Harry found out, as a useful anchor under which to wedge a sheet of newspaper so that it hung over the outside and provided shade for the young plants within.

Garden boys used to be able to carry large bell glasses three at a time – one over their head and one under each arm. It was a method, I'm told, which rendered them temporarily helpless! Glasses could range from 2 to 12 inches (2.5 to 30 cm) in diameter; unfortunately, not being of a substance impervious to accidents, few original ones remain. Also long since disappeared are the square wheelbarrows which, Harry remembers, the men working under glass used to have. These were generally made for them by the garden's carpenter and went through doorways far more easily than the conventional wide-ended ones used outside.

Glasshouse men used to keep their hand tools in the potting shed. Harry searched his old potting shed, now used more as a storehouse, and brought to light an unprepossessing collection. However, it turns out that these tools appeared thus even when 'new', for worn-down hoes and rakes with handles truncated by accident or design were just right to clear or smooth out sand or gravel on staging. Even worn besom brooms had their use, for dismembered heads could support potted Freesias. Well used but extremely serviceable were several zinc watering cans with spouts tipped with brass screw roses. The spouts were long and ideal for reaching pots of plants standing at the rear of staging.

A roll of blind made out of wooden slats was brought out of its resting place in the corner of the Peach house. Harry liked this old sort of glasshouse shading because he said it let in dappled light which did not scorch. Despite its merits, when unrolled and measured the piece of blind proved too narrow to be totally effective. To cover a useful area of glasshouse roof another was needed of equal size. David went to a local hardware shop and returned with a large quantity of 1-inch (2.5-cm) wooden laths and a ball of fine wire. He set up his workshop in the open-fronted pot-washing shed at the back of the garden wall. Two nails in the rafters provided a hold for the first lath which suspended from either end a long double trail of wire. The manufacture of the new blind progressed downwards. Each successive lath was placed between the double strands of wire at either end and secured by a twisting of the wires before these were opened out again to take the next lath. It was a job which required patience, certainly more than David had anticipated, for when it was finished and laid temporarily on a glasshouse roof, Harry, looking up at it from the inside of the house, declared that the slats were too far apart. Having used the old piece of shading as a guide, David was disappointed: it was obviously a case of an appearance having been deceptive. The new blind had to be dismantled and each lath set just a little bit closer. Harry approved it and it certainly worked better.

The new blind was heavier than the old and cumbersome to fix into place. Harry helped David and regaled everyone with stories of capers of the past when gardeners were told to put blinds back on the houses in spring. In fact the problems used to start the autumn before. This was when journeymen took them off the roof. The young men, with their term in a garden coming to an end and their thoughts on another garden and promotion, often didn't bother to mark which blind had been on which roof and just bundled them all into a shed. Come the spring, Harry says, there was hare and tear to get them back on the roofs and if they hadn't been correctly marked it was an unearthly job. Many glasshouses were built on site and so didn't run out to equal sizes, and if you didn't get the right blind on the right bay, you ended up with a gap or one blind overlapping another and that was no good because you couldn't roll it down properly. Straightening out the blinds had never been popular with Harry as he wasn't keen on clambering over glasshouse roofs. However, it had to be done, and he couldn't refuse when, as a young journeyman, he landed another roof job. He was put in charge of a house-washing gang. In those days glasshouses were washed inside and out every year. A foggy November morning was considered the ideal time to do the outside: it rendered dirt and algae wet and slimy enough to be moved easily with soft soap and water. It also rendered the task more hazardous, despite moving planks up on the roof as you went and resting them on nails driven into the main beams. Harry says the system was to start at the top and wash down, and as you got off a plank you moved it across to the next bay. He recalls being less than popular when, on one wet and greasy day, he let a plank drop through a large pane of glass on an orchard house.

There were no accidents on the day David's new blind was fixed and, although its wood looked a little 'new' in contrast to that of the old one next to it, the general opinion was that it would weather down. The general opinion was also that, successful though the venture had been, it would be too expensive and time-consuming to make any more blinds, and when, in the middle of April, some of the plants in the stovehouse began to show signs of stress, Harry began to consider other methods of shading. He chose whitening the panes with a venerable wash called Summer Cloud bought from a garden wholesaler. His predecessors would have done the same but would have made up their own mixture with equal quantities of whitening and skimmed milk. One thing was still the same: then, as now, whoever was applying the shading had to avoid the glasshouse woodwork as either mixture ruined white lead paint. Harry explained that whitened panes did the job of shading but didn't have the advantage of blinds which could be rolled up on dull days; if you had a long spell of dull weather, shading which was immoveable could cause drawn growth in the plants beneath. As matters turned out it wasn't a problem Harry had to face. The same hot sun that was scorching the herbaceous border outside spent the summer dappling through shading both wooden and whitened.

Three-quarters of the way down the show house, one on either side and sunk under the side staging, are two old concrete tanks. During the wet months these fill with rainwater which is channelled down from the roof guttering by ducts. The sides of the troughs are mossy and the water looks deep and green. It is an arrangement used in most old glasshouses and was thought to have several merits: it was convenient to anyone hand-watering, for there was little distance to travel to re-fill a watering can; being rain water it was free from lime and therefore ideal for acid-loving plants; and finally its temperature was thought to be correct because standing within the house it becomes nearly the same as that of the atmosphere. This used to be viewed as essential as nothing was considered more injurious to young roots or tender shoots of potted plants than to have cold water falling on them. Some houses even had the hot-water pipes passing through water reservoirs. If this wasn't so, it wasn't unknown for a man to take the chill off water by mixing it with some drawn off the pipes, although it was a frowned-upon practice because it caused air-locks. The belief in warm water was something Harry grew up with, for use not only on pot plants but also on greenhouse salad crops like cucumbers. He says that it was the Second World War which finally toppled the rule. With few available hands left to cope in gardens, it was too much trouble always to re-fill cans with warm water, and those whose job it was used what water was to hand, cold or otherwise. It was noticed that the cold water didn't seem to have any adverse effect.

Croton

Above: Begonia rex

Above right: Young Begonia plants beneath a bell glass

Right: Propagating by laying slit leaves onto compost

Concern with temperature had also affected old methods of potting. The maxim was to never re-pot plants in soil which had a much lower temperature than that of the house in which they were growing because it would be much too chilling for their roots. An effective method of heating the soil without drying it too much was to plunge hot bricks into it. Harry cannot remember this technique but does recall that the old wooden mobile potting benches, still at his gardens, were always moved into a particular glasshouse if there was something special in it to be re-potted. The fresh soil was taken in the day before to acclimatise it. As with warm water, this nicety was discontinued.

Pot tapping Harry still believes in. He thinks it is good training for anyone growing a mixed batch of plants. The doctrine is: if a quick rap with a wooden hammer evinces a dull thud from a pot, its contents are wet enough; if it provokes a ringing note, the plant needs a drink. Harry had learned this in the days when the watering of pot plants was done not as a routine but when each individual plant needed it. This might mean looking in on plants several times a day because one that had been damp enough, say, in the morning could be flagging by mid-day. He discovered that victims of sudden dehydration were most likely to be 'fillers' or interesting items in 5-inch (12.5-cm) pots. Anything in a large container like a climber usually needed looking at only once or twice a week. A foreman passing by and knowing that a lad had gone into the house to do some watering expected to hear the sound of the pot tapper. If it didn't assail his ears he usually went in to find out why.

Pot tapping, of course, couldn't be employed on hanging baskets and David had to assess the needs of those hung in the show house by climbing up to feel the soil. As the days became hotter a huge basket of lilac-coloured Achimenes became prone to drying out at an alarming rate.

A passing Arab, expressing the belief of his forebears that 'the Palm-tree has its roots in the water, and its head in the oven', would not have been disbelieved in the stovehouse. That is not to say, however, that the temperature in this hothouse had got out of hand – far from it. Harry was a past master at judging it and administering any necessary remedy. The stove plants liked humidity. This was achieved by dampening the floor and by liberal use on hot afternoons of a water syringe. In action this resembled a bicycle pump; in appearance it was somewhat vintage, with its wooden handle and fluted brass case. The syringe was a useful implement if you *knew* how to use it. It was easy enough to dip the end into a bucket of water and pull out the handle to suck water up inside, but it was getting the water out again which could pose a problem to the uninitiated. Any amount of vigorous pumping would result only in a miserable dribble. The secret was to make your index finger, on the hand that wasn't pumping the handle, into a pressure valve. Its application over and occasional release from the hole at the nozzle end could, with a good sweep of the arm, produce a spray as wide and, if the sun caught the droplets of water, as colourful as a peacock's tail.

Humidity wasn't just the result of employing water; it had also to do with ventilation. The importance of 'giving air' in glasshouses became apparent after nineteenth-century improvements in glazing. In the old days of small square panes there had been sufficient openings for currents of air, but with the new large sheets of glass there was no safety valve. Victorian gardening manuals carried reams of information on the subject. What bothy boy reading by candlelight could have failed to respond, as intended, to the poignant information that 'a plant condemned to pass its life in a still atmosphere is like nothing so much as a criminal set fast in an everlasting pillory'? On air and youth, William Taylor, head gardener at Longleat, Wiltshire, noted in a letter to the *Journal of Horticulture and Cottage Gardener* in March 1874: 'When a young gardener has learnt how to give air properly to plant and fruit houses he has, in my opinion, mastered the most difficult lesson in the whole of his very difficult profession . . .'

That Mr Taylor wrote in March is of consequence, for the time of year was then coming up to what Harry calls the two deadliest months for a journeyman under glass, April and May. Harry was taught to cope with the giving of air in these two months in what he reckons is the best training ground – a fruit range. Working in the range, he was shown how to put air on gradually. At first the ventilators were opened to 'a finger's depth', and as the temperature rose in the houses he kept floors or 'surrounds' damp and increased the air. If, as in those fickle months often happened, the sun went in suddenly and the temperature began to drop, he had to take the air down to a level which would keep the temperature in the houses correct. If the sun came out again, the air was put back on. A journeyman, Harry says, could in April and May be putting air on and taking it off umpteen times a day, and that included Saturdays, Sundays and bank holidays. Some days the sun would stay in long enough to take the outside temperature down to almost night-time level and on these days the houses would be shut up altogether.

The skill of balancing moisture and air gave, in Harry's words, 'a nice growing condition' inside a stovehouse, and he tried to maintain that in his newly restored one. It also discouraged insect pests and these he was anxious to avoid, especially as some plants were on loan. They can thrive if a stovehouse is very hot and dry, particularly the tiny red spider mite which absorbs sap and causes leaves to drop off. There is a fearful and colourful list of other possible invaders: white scale, brown scale, greenfly, yellowfly, mealy bug and thrips. The warmth inside a glasshouse lengthens their breeding season and unlike their brethren outside they are sheltered from natural predators, unless of course, as is sometimes the case today, a gardener introduces specially bought predators such as ladybirds. This idea of bringing predators into the house is by no means new, although it appears that in the past they were somewhat larger than ladybirds. Below are some helpful tips sent by a reader to *The Cottage Gardener and Country Gentleman* in 1858:

> I have heard lately from a neighbour (a good grower of stove plants) that the common greenplover, or peewit (by some also, called 'lapwing') is a very good friend to fanciers of stove plants for this reason – it will not peck or injure the plants; but will pick up everything in the shape of insect, be it what it may, that can be found in the house. At one time I was dreadfully worried with woodlice; for the last 4 or 5 months I have kept three hedgehogs (mother and two young ones) in my stove, and a woodlouse is a rarity.

Enterprise was not the province of men alone. A later edition published a letter from a lady who purchased a cheap glazed-calico crinoline for the purpose of dropping it down over infested vegetation. The crinoline became a fumigation tent which was left on overnight and removed next morning so that the job could be finished with a syringe.

It is quite likely that this lady used tobacco as her fumigating material. It could be smouldered in patent containers, or simply in a flower pot which had an additional hole knocked into the side, and was a standard Victorian remedy against aphids. Tobacco water, made by leaving strong shag tobacco in boiling water for a few hours, had the same effect if syringed on to plants. Alternative syringe mixes were water in which Quassia (a type of South American wood) chips had been steeped; soot and water (soot was seen as both an insecticide and a good fertiliser); or a combination of soft soap and petroleum jelly. If the latter were used, every second syringeful had to be squirted back into the bucket. This stopped oil collecting on the surface which could have led to some plants getting an unequal mix. For economy, a plant could be placed on a drenching board before being sprayed. The board caught and funnelled the insecticide into a bucket for re-use. Plants infested with red spider and too large for a drenching board had to be hand-sponged with tobacco water. Scale and mealy bug were kept at bay by sponging with hot soapy water and cleaning the plant's joints with a stiff brush.

Some gardeners attempted to knock aphids off when they syringed with ordinary water as part of the glasshouse 'damping-down' routine.

But this reckless deluging rather than 'dewing' of plants was seen as damaging to foliage. It was thought far better to go round with a pair of aphis brushes. These came in several designs, the most common being like a pair of scissors with a small soft-bristled brush on the end of each 'blade'. Beeton's *Aids to Gardening* (1890) describes their use: 'The brushes are closed on the infested shoot a little below the insects, and then drawn upwards and along it. Two or three applications of the brush will very nearly, if not entirely, remove all the aphids without doing any injury to the shoot.' In these anti-chemical days such brushes might make a re-appearance. Another eco-friendly bug remover once used in old private gardens was 1 lb (500 g) of rhubarb leaves boiled in 1 pint (700 ml) of water. The strained liquid was sprayed on to the foliage of pot plants to get rid of greenfly.

It seems fitting to end this chapter with one category of plant which draws together glasshouses, watering and insects. It also drew wonder from Victorian men of science for, according to one nineteenth-century account, these plants turned the tables on the normal. In a world where animals fed off plants, they fed off animals – or, to be precise, insects, although some Victorians did experiment and feed them bits of meat.

Harry's small but lethal collection of insectivorous plants managed their diet very well without such supplements. They existed in the summer months in the corner of a small, unheated but sunny glasshouse which formed part of the range adjacent to the show house. Harry knew them to be bog plants and set their pots in a shallow tray of rainwater, necessary because it was lime-free. As the summer brought drought, an emergency measure had to be implemented to keep up a supply of this commodity. Harry made a rule that the contents of a water butt outside the back door of his cottage must not be touched except to re-charge the insect-eaters' tray. It has to be admitted that this rule was mainly for himself and his wife, Jane. They normally cosseted little specialities in their own garden by waterings from the butt.

Most handsome and certainly most noisy of the insectivorous plants were tall Sarracenias. They are also known as Huntsman's Horn because each modified leaf looks like a graceful horn-like tube. At the summit the tube narrows and then fills out again to form a raised frilled precipice which overhangs the opening to the tube. Insects attracted by markings on the top of the foliage and its secretions fall off the lidded cliff top down into the tube. Despite their efforts they cannot climb back out and set up a desperate buzzing noise. Harry's Sarracenias were at their loudest when they trapped bees and they seemed to trap a lot. However large and numerous they were, all the trapped insects were eventually dissolved by enzymes and digested.

Sarracenia

Not so noisy but fatal to inquisitive flies were two Dionaea (Venus flytraps). Once flies alighted on their leaves, these traps closed and began the process of secreting a liquid which breaks down their prey. This liquid had fascinated nineteenth-century botanists. At first it was thought to come from the decomposing victim, but from a series of experiments which involved feeding Dionaea with bits of raw meat they concluded that the fluid came from the plant itself and acted like gastric juice. Its acidity was confirmed by an American, Mr Canby of Wilmington, Delaware, who, if *The Garden* of 1874 is to be believed, gave one of his Dionaea subjects fatal dyspepsia by feeding it with cheese.

Mr Canby was continuing pioneer work done by the English botanist Charles Darwin. Darwin's interest led him eventually to publish a book called *Insectivorous Plants* in 1875 which detailed his experiments and findings on insectivorous plants. Mr Canby's fatal cheese diet pales beside the substances Darwin administered to his Droseras (Sundews). He fed them with, among other things, bits of bone and chalk; and tried to poison them, with (*inter alia*) strychnine and snake venom. (He'd obtained the venom as powder from a Dr Fayrer who had studied cobras.) The Droseras stood up remarkably well to the poison but became temporarily insensible and unable to eat when given small doses of chloroform. Large doses of that substance proved fatal, as did turpentine and oil of Caraway. In addition to trying to ascertain the nature of their digestive power Darwin searched for an explanation of the sensitivity of their leaves by driving the points of lancets through them, pricking them with needles and dropping them into hot water. Perhaps it was all justified for, as *The New York Nation* (*circa* 1874) conjectured when musing on the question of why insectivorous plants take to organic food: 'What is the bearing of these remarkable adaptations and operations upon doctrines of evolution?'

What indeed? But on to Pinguiculas, of which Harry owned one. Smaller and more delicate than all the other insect eaters, it trapped its prey in a sticky fluid exuded from hairs on a rosette of pale succulent leaves. From May till July it bore a flower the shape and colour of a Violet. Harry was pleased to see the little Bog Violet, for it reminded him of a grand old Orchid grower he knew years ago. The man used to go to a piece of bog land near his nursery to collect Sphagnum moss which he needed as potting material for his Orchids. Unwittingly he often carried back embryo Pinguiculas hidden in the Sphagnum. When they sprang up out of the moss he would select the finest and grow them on in 3-inch (7.5-cm) pots. Harry cannot remember if he ever sold the Pinguiculas but says that they would have been useful plants to keep, for no one wanted flies in an Orchid house.

Dionaea (Venus flytrap)

CHAPTER SEVEN
The Orchid

Orchid subterfuge and hunters – Orchids as 'comforting' plants – The first hybrid – Cosseting – Mother pots – Mycorrhiza – Potting Cymbidiums – Mr Maule's strange Orchid pot.

Waterloo Station witnessed something of a to-do. It was at the platform from which the Southampton train was due to depart and it was on a day in 1880. A heated argument broke out between an intending traveller and the station master. The dispute was over some sacks the traveller was carrying. The station master demanded that they go by goods train, but the traveller said he didn't have time to organise this and that he was going to take them with him on to the waiting passenger train. A man already on the train leaned out to join in the argument and backed the traveller. The station master withdrew defeated and the man clutching his odd luggage climbed aboard. He was William Arnold, an Orchid hunter, and the contentious sacks contained Sphagnum moss. Arnold was on his way to try to find a Masdevallia orchid in Tovar, New Granada. If he found the Orchid in quantity, he would need the moss to keep the plants cool as they progressed by mule back from their natural high habitat through the hot regions to the port from which they would be shipped. Arnold was anxious to keep the sacks with him, for on this outward journey he had only one hour between the arrival of the train in Southampton and the departure of his ship. He turned gratefully to the helpful stranger who had espoused his cause at the station and when he learned that the man, who was named Thompson, was also journeying towards Caracas, Venezuela, and taking the very same ship, Arnold suggested that they share a cabin.

Mr Thompson's business was hardware but he had an enquiring mind for other people's affairs and on the boat journey he expressed interest in Orchids and Arnold's quest for the Masdevallia. The boat arrived at Caracas and, Thompson being particularly anxious to get away, the two men parted. Several hours later Arnold met his agent and the agent enquired whether he knew that an Orchid collector (an amateur who had turned professional) had started out for Tovar that very morning. Arnold's surprise that the man was in the country led the agent to exclaim, 'Why, as I understood, he travelled in the same ship as you.'

William Arnold

It didn't need great powers of deduction to realise who the rival Orchid collector was and, stopping only long enough to gather together a horse, a guide and a pistol, Arnold set off in pursuit. Fifteen miles along the road he found 'Thompson' about to take his supper in a roadside *posada*. Arnold barred the door and challenged him to get his pistol, but 'Thompson' disappeared beneath the table in fright. After hauling him out Arnold made him sign a confession and promise that he wouldn't revisit the district for six months, then for good measure sent him off supperless.

Arnold's tenacity in the face of authority at Waterloo Station had its reward. When he found *Masdevallia tovarensis*, of the plants he sent in his first consignment 40 000 arrived in England in good condition.

The quest for *Masdevallia tovarensis* is one of many ripping yarns that have become Orchid-hunting legends. The stories are laced with dangerous exploits and with the agonies the hunters endured, from wading thigh-deep through swamps for days on end to (perhaps most awful of all) being thrown, by outraged natives who revered Orchids, into temple pits already filled with live snakes. In the last quarter of the nineteenth century, when Orchids were big business, the majority of Orchid hunters were employed by nurserymen. William Arnold had been sent to Tovar by Frederick Sander, a nurseryman from St Albans. Sander, who was appointed Royal Orchid Grower by Queen Victoria, employed other famous collectors too, not the least of whom was Benedict Roezl. It is alleged that Roezl discovered 800 new species of plants during his career. In the latter years he concentrated on Orchids and on one expedition alone sent 8 tons of them to Europe. In addition to massive numbers, Orchids of great size were taken from their natural habitat. On one occasion F. W. Burbidge, who collected for Veitch & Son in Borneo between 1877 and 1878, secured a Grammatophyllum which was, according to contemporary accounts, 'as big as a Pickford's van and which a corvée of Dyaks could not lift'.

Veitch and Sanders were two of about half a dozen nurseries supplying a market imbued with the belief that no garden on a private estate was complete without its Orchid collection. This maxim had been nurtured on a bed of wonder brought about by the beauty and mystery attached to imported Orchids. In 1842 the *Quarterly Review* told readers:

It is scarcely more than 10 years ago that any particular attention was bestowed on this interesting tribe, and there are now more

Masdevallia tovarensis

Right: Phalaenopsis grandiflora *(a Moth Orchid –* phalaina *meaning 'a moth' and* opsis *meaning 'resemblance').* Phalaenopsis *were considered to rank among the most beautiful of stovehouse Orchids. The Victorian illustrator chose to team this example with* Correa cardinalis, *an elegant greenhouse shrub*

genera cultivated than there were then species known. . . . Among all the curiosities of botany there is nothing more singular . . . their manner of growth distinct from though so apparently like, our native Mistletoe and other parasitical plants – generally reversing the common order of nature, and throwing summersets with their heels upwards and head downwards . . .

The writer seems conveniently to have forgotten that not all Orchids are tree-dwellers (epiphytes) and that some grow on the ground. This may be because, compared to epiphytes, terrestrial Orchids were considered to be greatly inferior in beauty and singularity.

Novelty aside, it was also a better understanding of their culture which helped establish Orchid collections. Orchids had been cultivated in England since the eighteenth century. A species called *Bletia verecunda* was reputedly the first. It had been received from the Bahamas and bloomed in 1732. There are also records of the Vanilla Orchid being cultivated at botanical gardens. However, for the most part attempts to grow any Orchids sent from cool regions were doomed to failure as all types were treated the same – that is, they were plunged into tan pits in dry hothouses heated by flues. Joseph Paxton was the first gardener to experiment with glasshouses of differing temperatures for Orchids from different localities. His employer, the Duke of Devonshire, had begun a collection of Orchids in the 1830s. Paxton's apparent success led others to follow his example and instead of all Orchids being subjected to overheated stoves, it became the rule to divide them between 'cool', 'intermediate' and 'Warm or East India' houses. Successful culture was also aided by the constancy of temperature afforded by hot-water heating and a general improvement in construction. Some growers had their own ideas of a good Orchid house and builders followed their specifications.

There is an interesting late Victorian notion put forward by the writer Frederick Boyd that all this progress (introduction of Orchids, improvements in glasshouses, and so on) had all been ordained by the Creator. Indeed, that it was not unreasonable to believe that the beneficence Orchids conferred had been specifically designed from their inception to be withheld from civilised man until the latter half of the nineteenth century so that they could comfort the 'elect' of that 'anxious age'. Boyd had in mind particularly a Mr R. Measures who was told to rest by his doctor. Measures bought a house with 7 acres (2.8 hectares) at Streatham, then to the south of London, and from a chance purchase of a few pots of Orchids ended up with thirty-one Orchid houses under the watchful eye of the ex-Orchid foreman from Blenheim Palace and thirteen subordinates!

The anxieties of the Rt Hon Joseph Chamberlain, MP for West Birmingham, were also soothed by an Orchid collection. In the gardens of his house at Highbury, a suburb of Birmingham, he had thirteen glasshouses. These included a 'Flowering House' in which a representative selection of Orchids which were in blossom were staged. The majority of the houses opened off an impressive corridor which led from the mansion, enabling Chamberlain to view his Orchids without going out of doors. A special charge of his Orchid grower was the cultivation of the Odontoglossums, a handsome group of Orchids which gets its name from the tooth-like parts on the Orchid's lips. An Odontoglossum backed by a piece of delicate Maidenhair fern was one of Chamberlain's favourite buttonholes. The popularity of this particular Orchid among rich men for the lapel continued well beyond Chamberlain's time. Alan

A memorial card shows Chamberlain and his Orchids flanked by The Council House, Birmingham (left) and his house at Highbury (right)

F THE LATE Rt. HON. JOSEPH CHAMBERLAIN

N'S

GREATEST STATESMAN

Greatwood, a professional Orchid grower of forty-five years' standing, tells me that in his early days, when he worked for the Sussex Orchid nursery Charlesworth & Co., part of his job was to help dispatch, two or three times a week and to whichever residence or hotel he happened to be at, Odontoglossum buttonholes to the oil magnate Nubar Gulbenkian. Carrying a box by train and delivering it to the Ritz was an interesting diversion in Alan's week.

The majority of Orchids in Victorian collections were species. For many years no one knew how to raise a hybrid, and some considered this was part of the Orchid's charm. James Bateman of Knypersley Hall in Staffordshire, who was becoming well known as an Orchid cultivator in the 1830s, is recorded as having told the tale that his first Orchid-growing friend, a Mr Huntly, had pointed to the Cacti and Orchids at his rectory in Huntingdonshire and said: 'I like those plants, in fact they are the only plants I grow, because those fiends [meaning the hybridisers] cannot touch them.'

It was an Exeter surgeon named John Harris who set in motion the first Orchid hybrid. He suggested to John Dominy, an Orchid grower at Veitch & Son's Exeter nursery, the way in which he thought one Orchid could be crossed with another. Dominy followed his advice and the result, named *Calanthe* Dominii, flowered in October 1856. However, despite knowledge of the mechanics involved in obtaining them, the overall production of Orchid hybrids was slow. At the first Orchid Conference, held in the year 1885, the practice of hybridisation was described as being still in its infancy and the conference president, Sir Trevor Lawrence, admitted that it seemed to be far more difficult to raise the seedlings of some crossings than to raise very delicate children.

Young Orchids growing in a 'mother pot'

The problem appeared to lie with Orchid seed. An average-sized Orchid pod might give a dessertspoonful of extremely tiny seeds (there are examples of more accurate measurements: one pod of *Cymbidium tracyanum* was found to contain 825,000 seeds), but for all their number, few when inspected with a strong magnifying glass were found to be fertile. Those that were still posed problems for, despite being sown on various likely surfaces, such as blocks of wood, pieces of fern stem or strips of cork, their germination was poor. The simplest and most successful method (and which some attribute to John Dominy) was found to be sowing them on to the surface of a 'mother pot' – either that of the parent plant or one containing a full-grown Orchid which had been potted a few months previously so that the compost was 'sweet and sound'. Such pots were often placed beneath seed pods likely to burst so that there was no danger of losing the first seeds which were thought by some cultivators to be the most fertile.

It would take up to six months for seedlings to reach pin-head size and be ready for lifting out with a sharp-pointed stick prior to being pricked off into 1-inch (2.5-cm) pots. H. A. Burberry, writing in *The Amateur Orchid Cultivator's Guide Book* (1895), advised putting these pots into an Orchid basket and suspending them under the roof of the Orchid house but in a position protected from sun. Bearing in mind that, as a result of their size and elevation, the pots would dry out quickly, instructions for watering are also given – it is a gentle operation consisting of fingers dipped into water and then held to drip over the pots. Even after this degree of cosseting a succession of dull cloudy days in winter or a few hours of London fog could cause Orchid seedlings to perish.

Given the above troubles encountered in raising, it is no surprise to read an account of an unceasing watch being mounted at Veitch's nursery over a pot which contained the one and only successful seedling of a particular cross. A slug had eaten two of its three leaves and gone to ground in the pot. During the hours of the watch the surface of the pot was repeatedly ducked into water to encourage the slug's eventual appearance and removal.

Harry knows all about sowing Orchid seed on to 'mother pots' and describes a variation on this method. He recalls that, when he was a nipper at Blackmoor in the 1920s, his Uncle Fred used to go out to Lord Selborne's collection of conifers planted in the pleasure grounds and dig seedling conifers which had come up beneath them. He potted these up in the same soil in which they'd sprung up because he reckoned there was a natural Mycorrhiza in the soil which would keep them growing.

The word Mycorrhiza had been coined in 1885 by a scientist called A. B. Frank. He used it to describe the fungus Mycelia present in or around the roots of many plants and which, far from being detrimental, seemed to benefit both plant and fungus. As early as 1847 a German botanist called Reissek investigating fungi in the roots of flowering plants found that this fungus was best developed in the underground roots of Orchids. The knowledge of fungus in Orchid roots and the fact that it was difficult to germinate Orchid seed unless placed on Orchid soil led cultivators to suspect that the fungus played a part in seed germination. However, this wasn't confirmed until a Frenchman, Noel Bernard, who had started to study Mycorrhiza in 1899, published a thesis in 1902. It mentioned that Orchid seeds could germinate only in the presence of the root fungus and that the seedling was infected from its earliest stages: a beneficial infection, for a tiny Orchid seed carries little food and an embryo plant digests and gets nutriment from the threads of fungi. Bernard published a further paper in 1909 and in the same year he and an independent investigator succeeded in isolating the fungus from an Orchid root and growing it on a nutrient medium. Orchid seeds placed on to this germinated without difficulty.

Nurseryman Joseph Charlesworth, who was already dealing in Orchids, took up preparing culture flasks on a commercial scale and by 1913 was achieving remarkable results in raising Odontoglossum by what he told visitors was a 'pure culture method'. More formally the method is known as symbiotic, from the word symbiosis – the living together of two organisms in close association. In 1922 there was a further development. An American scientist invented the 'asymbiotic' technique of germinating seed, which involved sterilising seed and putting it on to sterile nutriment.

High science might have arrived but a certain mystery and elitism lingered on in Orchid cultivation right up to the Second World War. The perpetuators of these qualities were Orchid growers. Harry, who has worked in some very large private gardens, has come across such men. He owns that where a place had a varied collection of Orchids it needed a specialist to tend to their needs but also admits that Orchid growers could cause trouble. They usually considered themselves to be a cut above the rest of the men and the mystery of their art was kept because the general inside staff had very little to do with the Orchids. Harry says such men considered it an honour bestowed if they let you watch them make up Orchid compost for re-potting. As a pot boy he'd contributed to this ritual by pulling apart huge chunks of spiky Osmunda fibre. This was the root of the *Osmunda regalis*, a large fern which thrives in damp conditions. When it was lifted to store for later use in the compost, it was inevitable that the mud in which it had grown stuck to the roots. This meant that anyone pulling it apart at a later date got covered with dust or, if they were foolhardy enough to try damping down the dust, with sticky mud. Another contribution a pot boy made to Orchid potting was supplying the crocks which were stood on end in the bottom of the pot to give sharp drainage. He got the right shape and size for the crocks, Harry says, either by smashing pieces of broken flower pot with a hammer or by using a crock grinder. A grinder was the epitome of garden economy. Bits of broken pot fed into the hopper could be turned out in 1-inch (2.5-cm) squares suitable for crocking Orchid pots or, by the movement of a lever, the grinder could be made to chew pieces of pot almost as fine as dust. The fine grade was mixed into seed compost because it kept it moist enough to germinate seed but not wet enough to be waterlogged.

Some Orchids, Harry said, grew on a very spartan mixture, perhaps just Sphagnum moss and charcoal, but others needed a veritable cake mix. He thought that the best way of explaining how these were put together was to show how he remembered a Cymbidium mix being prepared. The ingredients were: Osmunda fibre; bracken chopped up into 3-inch (7.5-cm) pieces; oak leaves; charcoal (for 'sweetening') and Sphagnum moss teased out like the Osmunda. Each was laid one on top of the other on a potting bench. Harry explained that if he were making enough mixture to pot a large number of Orchids, he would turn the ingredients with a fork, but as it was only a small amount he turned it with his hands. He then went back through it, making sure that every bit was distributed evenly through the pile. The next step was to make it moist, using enough water to go through the heap and wet the leaves. This watering also meant that the roots of any freshly potted plant would have a chance to start to enter the new compost before it needed watering again. If potting went on over several days, Harry said, a piece of damp hessian was put over the waiting mixture to keep the moisture in.

Potting wasn't going to go on for several days, although Harry did have several Cymbidiums in the garden. In fact, tucked away in odd corners, he had a few choice specimens of different Orchids that he'd tended for years. Most were suited to cool houses and every so often a beautiful flowering Orchid seemed to materialise from nowhere and appear on the show house staging. Although most of the Orchids were in wide pans or ordinary large flower pots, one was in a pot perforated about its sides with holes 1 inch (2.5 cm) in diameter. Pots of this nature had once been fashionable among Orchid growers because they accommodated the air roots, but by the 1880s these pots began to fall from favour because it was thought that they harboured insects.

When Harry finished off his demonstration, showing in what mixture and how a Cymbidium used to be potted, he used neither an ordinary pot, nor one with holes, but Mr Maule's flower pot. This had arrived at the garden a few weeks previously and was an extraordinary object; but then, Mr Alexander Maule had been a man of unusual calibre. He had inhabited a plant nursery which was described on his death in 1884 as 'an old-fashioned, all-round establishment'. Ten years prior to Mr Maule's demise a journalist had called at the nursery and later recorded for the *Gardener's Chronicle* how difficult the conditions there were for outdoor plant growing. Looking around, he had seen a colliery or two within rifle shot; the chimneys of Bristol close at hand and encircling, and even a pottery on the premises!

When quizzed, Mr Maule had appeared sanguine in the face of these adversities. The smoke he saw as a disinfectant which kept maladies at bay and the pottery was used to fashion flower pots to his own design.

Above: Orchid seeds as fine as grains of flour

Left: The crock grinder converting broken pieces of flower pot into powder

Below: A Lady's Slipper (Cypripedium). Ease of cultivation and a long flowering period made the commoner forms of this Orchid popular amongst amateurs

*Above: Mr Maule's Orchid pot
planted up*

Right: The Cymbidium flowers

Although this isn't recorded, perhaps there was an unconscious link between the surroundings and Mr Maule's designs, for he grew his large Orchids in, as the journalist wrote for the delectation of his readers,

... tall, rough, stump pots, perforated with numerous apertures. The plant is placed at the top of these pots, in a mixture of leaf-mould and fibre, with bits of charcoal intermixed, and is never disturbed. . . . It must be admitted that at first these large pots, looking like distorted chimney-pots, have not a very inviting appearance; but by-and-bye, as the plant grows, and the pots themselves get covered with seedling ferns, with *Ficus repens*, or other vegetation, this disagreeable appearance is done away with.

Almost a hundred and twenty years after the above was noted, Mr Maule's nursery had another interested visitor, a garden historian researching the man and keen to see the site of his one-time business. The premises, no longer surrounded by smoking chimneys or collieries, traded as a nursery until a few years ago but the present incumbent has now retired. Although not connected with Mr Maule who died a bachelor, she comes from a long line of nurserymen and naturally the garden around the house is kept trim. For years it has had, by way of useful ornament, two tall strange-looking flower pots. One is filled with a plant; the other, much frailer and with a part of the base missing, stands empty. Needless to say, once observed, the significance of these 'stump pots' was not lost on the garden historian and by a circuitous route and because the lady owner approves of Harry, the empty pot was kindly loaned for our Orchid re-potting.

With a Cymbidium standing by awaiting its new place of abode, Harry filled Mr Maule's pot with the Orchid compost. Out of reverence for the pot's antiquity he forbore to ram the mixture down tight as the old Orchid growers had taught him to do. It used to have to be pushed in so hard, he said, that the dibber he used brought the middle of his hand up in blisters. The compost seemed secure enough without this drastic treatment, and with the Cymbidium in place Harry pricked into the compost surface some live heads of Sphagnum moss, remarking that if the conditions were right we would soon be able to see the Orchid roots growing out into it.

A little bemused by the pot's other orifices and perhaps, like the journalist all those years ago who considered it only acceptable when camouflaged, Harry decided to put pieces from a Coelogyne Orchid and some small Paphiopedilums in the holes around the pot's middle sections. As a finishing touch he set pieces of fern in the bottom holes where it was too low to put anything that would hang down.

Had Mr Maule, in the days when Orchids were sent to bless the 'elect', been the last person to have dressed the pot so fine? It was quite likely. The longevity of the pot suited its occupant for, unless ill-treated, Orchids will regenerate indefinitely.

CHAPTER EIGHT

The Rose

*Roses on Sundays – Briar hunters – The Rose house at Chilton – Tea Roses –
Bowing to 'Gloire de Dijon' – Noisettes – Bourbon opulence – Hybrid
Perpetuals and a verse to one – The first Rose show – Harry's Rose culture,
including 'pegging' – Rosariums – Ramblers – Harry buds his standards.*

Victorian sermons could last for several hours – a useful length of time to a Rose grafter once employed by Mr Maule (of Orchid pot fame). During the week the Rose man's fingers became filled with thorns, but he didn't waste time taking them out daily. He bore them patiently until sitting in church on Sunday, when, according to Mr Maule:

as soon as the parson gave out his text, he took his penknife from his pocket, and, under the genial influence of a soothing discourse, he quickly and deliberately drew the prickly invaders from his fingers, and returned home with clean hands to begin another week of budding and grafting next morning in a dutiful frame of mind.

If the Lord's day was a good one for thorn extraction, it was in 1877 viewed as suitable for the introduction of the shrub which bore them. Between the years 1854 and 1877 a survey had been carried out to ascertain how many new Roses were introduced each year. The average was found to be fifty-two, or one a week. A suggestion arose that, if admitted on a Sunday, each new Rose would provide a refreshment for the blessed day of rest.

Where did all these new Roses come from? For the most part they came from France, but as the nineteenth century progressed English-raised Roses found a ready market. Although fewer in number compared with the French ones, the new English Roses generally displayed a better quality. This was put down to the fact that, unlike the French, most had passed the scrutiny of floral committee experts or show judges before appearing in catalogues.

The first Rose catalogue ever published by an English grower appeared in 1833. An imperial folio sheet which could be sent in the post as a single letter, it listed almost 500 varieties and was written by Thomas Rivers, a nurseryman from Sawbridgeworth in Hertfordshire.

Right: 'Souvenir de la Malmaison' (blush-pink) and 'Général Jacqueminot' (red) illustrated in The Gardener's Assistant, *1859*

Left: Evening sunshine in the Rose house at Chilton

Rivers' reason for publishing the catalogue was partly to clear up confusion over names of French Roses. The year 1837 saw the publication of his book, *The Rose Amateurs Guide*, which was regarded as the first practical work on the Rose and ran to eleven editions. Rivers stated that he had based it on the knowledge he'd gained from growing Roses for over twenty years on a larger scale than anyone in Europe. On 5–6 acres (2–2.4 hectares) at his nursery he had 100 000 Roses. The nursery, which also grew fruit trees, had been in the Rivers family since 1725.

When Thomas was a young man learning his trade, standard Rose trees had all been imported from France, the country credited with having introduced this method of growing Roses. London nurseryman Lee of Hammersmith was the first to bring them into England in 1818. He sold them at 1 guinea (£1.05) a piece and it is reported that the Duke of Clarence gave him an order for a thousand trees. Exporting standard Rose trees into Britain became a lucrative business for Paris and Rouen nurserymen. The youthful Rivers, aware of this, began experiments to find alternatives to imported standards. After an initial failure he turned his attention to the ready-made standards of the Dog Roses he saw in woods and hedges. He brought so many back to the nursery that the old foreman who had been with the family for three generations protested: 'Master Tom, you'll ruin the place if you keep on planting them rubbishy Brambles instead of Standard Apples!' These fears were not justified however, for the tall wild briars proved successful stocks for standard Roses.

Although some Rose lovers decried standard trees (one likened them to monkeys mounted on giraffes), they were valued for giving form and height to a display and their popularity increased to such an extent that a garden manual published in 1884 noted: 'Many attempts have been made of late years to laugh these tall Roses down. But it seems they only increase the faster. They appear to thrive on ridicule, and only to "take in" additional fields of farms, the more keen and sharp the ridicule becomes.' The 'taking in' of fields was to accommodate the finds of the briar-hunting trade (a far cry from the young Thomas Rivers' early forays for wild briars). To supply a massive Rose industry, individuals armed with sharp mattocks scoured woods and hedges all over the country. These 'briar men' collected tens of thousands of wild Rose briars. On some railway lines the truck-loads of briars heading for nurseries between November and December equalled the number of trucks of coal.

It was not a trade viewed with affection by gamekeepers who had good reason to try to keep their pheasants undisturbed during the shooting season. In 1879 the Duke of Buccleuch's gamekeeper, a Mr

Rose(!), gave evidence at Rugby magistrates' court to support an allegation of the theft of £150 worth of briars. It was an interesting test case, for a briar wasn't a tree or sapling, and a local farmer called as a witness said that as far as he was concerned a briar was a weed and a nuisance. Despite this opinion, the culprit was fined £1 10s (£1.50) and ordered to pay costs.

Herbie Norgate, who worked as a propagator on the Blackmoor estate where Harry was brought up, used to collect Rose briars though not in excess. He did it as a sideline and got enough to fill a bed in front of his estate cottage. The cottage was by the road and when the wild stocks had been budded with garden Roses and were in bloom, they were their own advertisement and he had a ready sale. As a boy Harry used to peer over Herbie's fence and admire these Roses. Before he left school

A Carter's nursery field filled with standard Roses

CARTERS' ROSE FIELDS.

During the Royal Visit to the Royal Agricultural Society's Show at Norwich,

JAMES CARTER & CO., H.R.H. the Prince of Wales's Seedsmen,

HAD THE HONOUR OF

Presenting to H.R.H. THE PRINCESS OF WALES

A VERY HANDSOME BOUQUET OF ROSES FROM MESSRS. CARTERS' ROSE GROUNDS IN KENT.

SPECIAL NOTICE.—The County of Kent (in which our Nurseries are situate) is familiarly known as The Garden of England, and the soil and climate are specially adapted for the growth of Roses to the greatest perfection.

OUR STOCK OF ROSES COMPRISES ONLY THOSE VARIETIES INCLUDED IN THE ROSE ELECTIONS AS THE VERY BEST.

The Collection of 24 varieties (our Selection), price **40**s. | The Collection of 12 Varieties (our Selection), price **21**s.

he got to learn the art of budding, but not from Herbie, nor from Rose stocks. He learned it by watching men in the field behind his cottage working on fruit stocks. The estate was trying to build up its complement of fruit trees and the budders, who were on piece-work, went so fast that their action was a source of wonder to Harry. They sped from one stock to another, leaving the bud to be tied in by women following in their wake.

Harry holds briar stocks in high esteem. He says that although they can be more difficult than cultivated stocks, once you've got a Rose established on one it goes on and on. He points to a prolific example in his garden called 'Shot Silk' budded on to a briar probably about sixty-five years ago, but looking nowhere near retirement.

Dog Rose

Thrashed by tractor-driven cutters, the hedges around Harry's present estate seemed too neat to yield Dog Roses. Nevertheless, one weekend in the early part of the year, having conjured them from somewhere, he brought a bundle of tall briars into the kitchen garden. Each was roughly 6 feet (1.8 m) tall and the thickness of a man's finger. He planted them in a businesslike row running north to south and parallel with a row of espalier fruit trees trained against the fence skirting the right-hand vegetable quarter. It was a neat, unobtrusive position and would be the briars' home for many months. The time to bud them was from mid-summer onward and until that time, apart from making sure that they weren't being rocked by the wind and that they had water if March turned out to be dry, they would want little attention.

It was as well, for Harry had his mind on other Roses, those he was planning to plant under glass, for Chilton, unlike any other large garden Harry has worked in, possesses that nineteenth-century status symbol – a Rose house. To have such a house in that era and not have to rely on getting cut Roses from a conservatory or orchard house signified taste and opulence. When Harry first saw the Rose house in 1947, it was catering for taste in another form, being full of vegetable crops grown for war food production. But men who had worked at the gardens in the years before Harry's arrival assured him that right up until the outbreak of war the house had lived up to its name and had been solid with Roses. Climbers had scrambled on supports beneath the roof glass and others, planted in a rear border, had covered the back wall. Beneath them the main body of the house had been filled with Roses in pots.

Now, asked for the television series to put the Rose house back to something like its former glory, Harry was checking modern Rose catalogues to see if any of the nineteenth-century varieties that might once have been grown there were still being sold. Tea Roses were a priority. The first ones had arrived in Britain from Canton in 1810. So named because of their tea-like perfume, they were valued in Victorian gardens for their delicate colours and because they responded well to forcing. The latter quality also made them favourites with nineteenth-century market gardeners. In the late 1870s, over the winter months, one Bexley Heath market gardener sent from 70 dozen to 200 dozen Tea Rosebuds to market every morning. They were always cut from the glasshouses during the previous afternoon by a man accompanied by a boy. The man went over the pots cutting off suitable blooms and placed them on a large shallow tray balanced on the boy's head. From the market the Roses found their way to florists and street vendors who, around Christmas, could charge up to 2s 6d (12½p) for a single bloom. For that money the purchaser would most likely have got a 'Niphetos' (pure white) or an 'Isabella Sprunt' (golden yellow), two varieties of Teas valued by market gardeners as profuse bloomers.

'Isabella Sprunt' appeared to have had her day, for no Rose of that name was listed in modern catalogues, but plants of 'Niphetos' could still be purchased. Other Tea Roses still available were 'Safrano' (saffron-yellow, 1839); 'Adam' (peach-pink, 1833); and 'Gloire de Dijon' (buff or salmon-yellow, 1850). These three had been recommended in an article entitled 'Roses All the Year Round' written in 'The Garden' in 1874. Taking it that the advice given in the article was still sound, Harry marked them off for purchase. He particularly liked the idea of having 'Gloire de Dijon'. It was hardier than most Teas and was, he said, the Rose which you often found growing against old stable blocks. It also apparently had a reputation for covering church towers. Cassell's *Popular Gardening* states that it will climb to the top of the highest tower in an incredibly short time and Reynolds Hole, the 6-foot-3-inch Victorian

Left to right: Tea Roses, 'Niphetos', 'Adam' and 'Gloire de Dijon'

clergyman who was as obsessed with Roses as any man could be, had 'Gloire de Dijon' growing on the chancel wall of his church at Caunton, Newark, Nottinghamshire. He wrote that it had two hundred flowers on it 'in full and simultaneous bloom' and that he shouldn't be accused of superstitious practices when he made a daily obeisance to it, for 'I only duck to preserve my eyesight.'

In addition to Tea Roses old journals recommended that Rose houses should have a few 'superior Noisettes'. These Roses first came about, it is thought, as the result of a natural cross between the *Rosa chinensis* (sometimes called *Rosa indica* because it was brought from China via the East India Company) and *Rosa moschata*, a musk-scented species. They originated in America and were so named because a Philippe Noisette sent some to his brother, a Parisian florist, in 1815 or 1819. Working from what Victorian Noisettes were still available, Harry reckoned that 'Mme Alfred Carrière' (pinkish-white, 1879), 'Aimée Vibert' (small double white, 1841) and 'Maréchal Niel' (golden-yellow, 1864) were sufficiently superior. As he planned to plant both the front and the back of the Rose house with climbers, he bulked up his order list by including 'Zéphirine Drouhin' (cerise-pink, 1868) and 'Souvenir de la Malmaison' (blush pink, *circa* 1843). Both are Bourbon Roses, and if a Rose house was once thought to have symbolised opulence, Bourbons, with their heavy cup-shaped blooms and rich scent, could not have been a more fitting choice. They were the result of a chance cross on the French Isle of Bourbon in about 1817 between *Rosa chinensis* and a Damask Rose (cultivated since Roman times).

A glance down Harry's list showed that the colours of the Roses chosen so far were delicately pale. It was an unavoidable circumstance, for most Teas and Noisettes are light-coloured. Some strong colours were needed for contrast and to get them it seemed sensible to do what nineteenth-century gardeners had done: add some Hybrid Perpetuals. In addition to darker colours these Roses, as their name suggests, had another characteristic which endeared them to Victorians. Unlike most old sorts of Roses, which bloomed only in summer, they flowered from spring to autumn. They were the result of the Bourbon Rose being crossed with other kinds including Damasks and *Rosa chinensis*, and the first of note was 'La Reine', produced by a French grower in 1842. There were three particular Hybrid Perpetuals, each a different shade of crimson, which had been rated highly in their day and which were still available. Harry put all three on his list. They were 'Charles Lefebvre' (1861), 'Duke of Edinburgh' (1868) and 'Général Jacqueminot' (1853) – the last named after one of Napoleon's generals. In 1895 a poetess called Bessie Chandler, overcome with the romance that the man's exploits had become forgotten but that everyone knew the Rose, wrote

Ah! the fate of a man is past discerning!
 Little did Jacqueminot suppose,
At Austerlitz or at Moscow's burning,
 That his fame would rest in the heart of a rose!

I doubt that the General, had he known, would have minded this fate at all, particularly as the Rose was to be favoured as a hair ornament by Victorian ladies with dark tresses.

Hybrid Perpetuals, owing to their hardiness and repeat flowering, were also much favoured in outside borders. Dark crimson sorts or rose and pink colours were seen as ideal for 'massing'. Perpetuals became so popular that a correspondent to the *Journal of Horticulture and Cottage Gardener* in May 1877 complained of their ever-increasing power. Gone, he said, were the old summer Roses once found in catalogues; in their place was 'a preponderance everywhere of Hybrid Perpetuals, Bourbons and Teas'. He placed the blame for the rise of this triumvirate on their popularity as exhibition blooms at Rose shows. If that were truly the case, the blame in turn must rest on the Reverend Reynolds Hole for, concerned at the fact that 'even the vulgar hairy Gooseberry' had an exhibition of its own but the Rose did not, it was he who set about organising the first Rose show. Helped by Rose nurserymen Thomas Rivers, Charles Turner and William Paul, Hole obtained his desire on 1 July 1858 when more than 2000 people turned up at St James's Hall, London, to view Roses from half the nurseries of England. It was a glorious day for the Reverend, the only slight jar being that the music of the Coldstream band specially hired for the occasion proved 'too loud for indoor enjoyment'.

Reynolds Hole had been a great believer in farmyard manure for Roses. He likened the liquids which drained from it to rich gravies from a baron of meat. Harry is an equal believer. When all the Roses for the Rose house had been purchased, those to be planted in the front and back borders were each given a hole roughly 3 feet by 2 feet (1 m by 60 cm) and 2 feet (60 cm) deep, bottomed out with farmyard manure. As an extra incentive to growth, half a barrel-load of fresh soil was substituted for that which had been dug out; a quantity of hoof and horn was added and a mulch of farmyard manure put on top when the Rose was in place. The Roses in pots, once they had put on about a foot (30 cm) of growth, were treated weekly to liquid manure. This had been made by soaking a bag of cow manure in a tank of water for a few weeks. The water turned a deeply interesting colour and required diluting to the shade of weak tea before being administered. As the year progressed the dosage grew more potent – it was now the colour of strong tea – and was put on twice a week. The border Roses also received liquid manure when it was felt they had exhausted their manure mulch.

Despite careful shading and airing, the Rose house seemed prone to mildew and a grey film began to appear on the leaves of many of its inmates. Particularly affected was 'Souvenir de la Malmaison'. In retrospect Harry thought that perhaps this was because it was on the back wall very near the entrance door. The door opened inwards and on very warm days when it was propped open it unavoidably shut in the old 'Malmaison'.

Harry said the mildew wasn't anything out of the ordinary. In the old days affected parts had been dusted with Flowers of Sulphur which was left on for a day or two. As Harry had a packet of Flowers of Sulphur powder and the wherewithal to apply it, he set about the job. His applicator was a hybrid between a pair of bellows and a watering can. Pumping the bellows moved a lever which released a flow of yellow sulphur from the can and the air from the bellows blew the sulphur down a long spout which terminated in a flat piece of metal. The flattened end helped to diffuse the sulphur into a cloud rather than a straight jet. This useful tool rejoiced in the trade name Perfecta and had seen sixty years of service.

Although Harry had been sanguine about the mildew, before it was treated it had looked unsightly, and it is easy to see why Hybrid Teas had failed to become accepted when they were first introduced. They were crosses between Hybrid Perpetuals and Teas, and early ones with a stronger strain of the latter proved disappointingly prone to mildew. The first had been 'La France', raised in 1867, but Hybrid Teas did not become universally popular until the turn of the century when breeding had ironed out the mildew problem.

Talking about the Rose house one day, Harry said that a piece of ground immediately in front of it, which stretched right down to the north-facing wall of the kitchen garden, had once been a formal Rose garden. If Reynolds Hole's maxim regarding the positioning of outside Roses – 'Expose to the morning's sunshine, protect from cutting winds' – is to be believed, the placing of the formal Rose garden on the eastern side of the kitchen garden at Chilton had been sensible. The mansion commands a fine view but its elevated position can make the surrounding pleasure grounds windswept. Harry's severely tried sub-tropical bed bore witness to this. However, Harry *did* plant some Roses by the mansion. He cheated the elements by following the old practice of pegging the shoots of the Roses down. He cut the pegs from nut sticks, leaving one limb of each hook longer than the other so that it could be pushed

Above: Noisette 'Maréchal Niel'

Above right: Bourbon 'Zéphirine Drouhin'

Right: Hybrid Perpetual 'Duke of Edinburgh'

Far right: Hybrid Tea 'La France'

into the ground. He pegged the Roses over a warm south-facing slope with the object of making them form a carpet of foliage and flowers. Thomas Rivers had been the first person to advise this terrestrial method of growing climbers.

Victorian landowners with pleasure grounds which had suitably sheltered spots could, and did, have some very grand Rose gardens, referred to as 'rosariums'. There is a fine example of one at Warwick Castle. Designed in 1868 by the eminent landscape architect Robert Marnock, this rosarium had, all but the site, disappeared. However, Paul Edwards, a consultant landscape architect working at the castle, discovered Marnock's original plans and masterminded a re-building. The restored garden, complete with iron arches, arbours, tripods and rails supporting rambling and climbing Roses, was opened to the public in 1986. Among all its Roses it would be fitting to find the one called 'Robert Marnock', introduced in 1877 by the Cheshunt Rose nursery Messrs Paul & Son, but like Mr Marnock's original garden this particular rose has probably long since disappeared.

The restored rosarium at Warwick Castle

In the last decade of the nineteenth century isolated formal Rose gardens fell from favour and Roses began to weave their way in among the flowers and trees of the rest of the garden. This move had been helped by the introduction from Japan of *Rosa multiflora* and *Rosa wichuraiana*, two Roses which led to an improvement in ramblers. Writing of *R. multiflora Grandiflora*, Gertrude Jekyll likened using a long-forked stick to direct its growth among the branches of a tree, to painting a picture with an immensely long-handled brush. An artist and pioneer of using Roses as furnishings, Miss Jekyll would have appreciated Harry's description of the ramblers which grew at Nuneham Park near Oxford almost half a century ago. Harry had arrived at Nuneham as a garden foreman. He remembers an enormous border in the garden which had in it conifers cut off to stumps of 12 to 15 feet (3.6 to 4.5 m) in height. The branches of these trees were cut to varying lengths and Roses planted either side had their shoots trained up through them. It was, he says, the finest example of rambling Roses he'd ever seen.

In mid-July Harry ran a test on one of the wild briar stocks to see if, when he made a small cut in it, the bark lifted easily. It did. He went to the Rose house and selected a shoot from a 'Gloire de Dijon' on which the flowers were just fading. At the base of the leaves it had several good prominent buds which he felt would do us proud. He trimmed back the leaves on it. While he was preparing the stock he kept the shoot moist by standing it in a small container of water. Eugene Delamer, writing in 1860 in his book *The Flower Garden*, had suggested that single buds could be kept moist in the budder's mouth and helpfully added that budding should be like a surgical operation: quick to spare the patient's sufferings. Having learned from the Blackmoor piece-workers, Harry was quick. He mad a 'T' cut in the bark on the wild briar stock, being careful not to cut the wood beneath, then, stooping to the shoot resting in water, he cut off a bud complete with a sliver of bark and its attached leaf stalk. With the end of the bud facing to heaven he pushed it between the 'T'-cut bark and on to the sticky surface of the wood beneath, then immediately wound it round with wet bass (raffia). The purpose of leaving the leaf stalk was, he said, because it acted as an indicator. If, after a week or two, it fell off when it was touched, the bud had 'taken', but resistance to dropping meant that the bud had shrivelled and died.

The buds did 'take' but it will probably be next year before the garden sports its new batch of 'Gloire de Dijon'. By that time too Harry reckons that the climbers in the Rose house will start to show the benefit of what went into the bottom of their beds. Both sights are worth waiting for.

CHAPTER NINE
Cut Flowers

*Laying out a cut-flower plot – Intricacies of the Gladiolus – No Double
Rocket – Carnations, both border and Malmaison – Henry Eckford, the father
of the Sweet Pea – the Dahlia – Mrs Barrett remembers 'The Bishop' –
Chrysanthemums and 'dressing' them.*

Tea Roses cut from a Rose house in the dim
months of November and December proved invaluable to Victorian head gardeners trying to furnish bouquets for ladies. This requirement for cut
flowers, not only for bouquets but also to decorate
rooms and tables at the mansion, went on all year.
In many gardens the demand became heaviest from
the months of mid-summer onwards when, with the London season at
an end, the family returned to the country. To meet the demand, gardeners could not take flowers from the decorative beds and borders
around the mansion: the number required would have destroyed the displays. Instead, it was customary to set aside a plot of ground, often in the
walled kitchen garden, and plant it up with flowers suitable for cutting.
The supply which could be gained from such a plot was, according to the
garden journalist William Robinson, 'equal to that of twenty plant
houses'. He saw the plot being prepared as a market gardener would
treat it, well enriched and in 4-foot (1.2-m) beds. Harry also saw it as
market gardening. He said that, in his experience, cut flowers for the
mansion had to be done on a mini-commercial scale otherwise there
would be nothing like enough, and he preferred to lay the flowers out in
long straight rows, 1 or 2 feet (30–60 cm) apart. For his cut-flower plot
he selected a piece of ground where the rows, edged by a cordon of Goose-
berries, would run down the left-hand quarter of the kitchen garden.

In March, when conditions were such that Harry described them as
perfect, with 'a bit of dust' which was lovely to see, the ground for his
cut-flower plot worked down until it felt like velvet underfoot. With an
eye to providing colour for vases during the winter months he sowed
seeds of the flowers Victorian ladies knew as 'Immortelles', the everlasting Helichrysum, Statice and Acroclinium. Other seedlings placed in line
were China Asters and Rudbeckias. Knowing that mansions have some
extremely large vases, Harry also planted plenty of Larkspur. He said it

gave masses of light feathery flowers. He had sown it the previous autumn and over-wintered it. The resultant seedlings had been planted out at intervals of 6 inches (15 cm) in rows a foot (30 cm) apart. There were sufficient left to plant up a patch in front of the old vineries too.

Such odd patches of garden were handy places for cut flowers, and sheltered along the back of another glasshouse a useful cut flower was already well established. It was *Gladiolus byzantinus*, originally from Turkey, though there are records of its being grown in Britain as long ago as 1629. Harry's particular patch was venerable in its way. It had been planted, he believed, by his late Victorian predecessor, Charles Beckett. Harry said that *G. byzantinus* was valued not for its beauty – indeed, some might think its maroon flowers dull – but for its early blooming. Several Gladioli which did combine beauty and earliness for cutting, each in a pot afforded warmth and shelter by the Rose house, were already on the point of flowering. One was *Gladiolus colvillei* or, to be exact, a white sport of that sort called 'The Bride' and introduced by a London nursery in 1827. There were also pots of other early kinds: 'Blushing Bride', a partially reverted pinkish form of 'The Bride'; and, not quite such an age but chosen because they had the same origins, 'Spitfire' and 'Nymph'. Ron Park of the British Gladiolus Society had advised that these would not look out of place in a Victorian glasshouse. For examples of the old sort of large-flowered summer Gladiolus that would have bloomed outside in a cut-flower plot he advised several sorts, but a check through modern catalogues revealed that only two were still readily available. These were 'Snow Princess' (white) and 'Hunting Song' (red).

The story behind the advent and progress of the large-flowered Gladiolus is worth telling, if only to allow us to marvel at its complexities. It is supposed to have begun in 1837 when a tall large-flowered Gladiolus was raised in Belgium by the Duke of Arenberg's gardener. He sent it to a Ghent nurseryman, named Van Houtte, for distribution. It was called *Gladiolus gandavensis* (Latin for 'of Ghent'). In 1853 Queen Victoria visiting Paris saw *G. gandavensis* and asked for some to be sent to her gardener at Osborne House on the Isle of Wight. From Osborne *G. gandavensis* was sent to Kew and eventually became distributed around Britain. John Standish, a grower from Bagshot, was entrusted with seeing that the corms from Paris got to Osborne House. The tale goes, however, that Standish had made similar crosses and had his *own* hybrids which he slipped into the consignment for Osborne. This is backed up by reports that some of the *G. gandavensis* which eventually bloomed at Osborne had never been seen in France!

However, quite a different story relating to the origins of *G. gandavensis* is brought to light by an article in the *Journal of Horticulture*

Previous pages: Harry in the cut-flower plot gathering flowers for drying

and Cottage Gardener for 10 September 1861. Replying through its pages to a letter received from Charles Darwin, Donald Beaton states that this variety is an English seedling raised by Dr William Herbert and J. T. Alcock. These two couldn't flower it or any of the seedlings of the same cross, so sent them to a Mr Bidwell in Sydney, Australia, 'where the climate was more favourable'. Mr Bidwell flowered all the seedlings and one of them, *G. gandavensis*, found its way back to Europe.

James Kelway

The person who first started to hybridise and improve *G. gandavensis* was M Souchet, a gardener to the French Court at Fontainebleau. In 1857 an English nurseryman, James Kelway, obtained through Souchet's Paris agents all the best varieties that the Frenchman had raised. He planted them and in the following year collected, as he recalled in later years, 'a tolerable quantity of seed'. Kelway reckoned that the best time to cross one Gladiolus with another was ten o'clock in the morning on a dry day. It is obvious that he met with success, for by the 1870s Kelway & Son's annual Gladiolus catalogue was listing the names and descriptions of almost 800 kinds. The Kelways had at that time 8 acres (3.2 hectares) of Gladiolus at their nursery, 6 (2.4 hectares) filled with plants in bloom and 2 (0.8 hectare) filled with seedlings. A suitably impressed correspondent from the *Gardeners' Magazine* wrote: 'No words of mine can convey anything approaching an adequate idea of the grand effect produced by the thousands of gladioli in bloom at the time of my visit.'

When it was exhibited at horticultural shows, the grandeur and brilliance of *G. gandavensis* earned James Kelway and his son William many awards. The date on which they could generally cut the finest blooms was 25 August, and hopes must have been justifiably high when father and son travelled to a London show on 23 August 1875. But glory can sometimes be prefaced by frustration, as a curiously modern-sounding entry in James Kelway's diary for that day shows: 'Self and Wm. by G. Western to Alexandra Palace, got there about 6 p.m. by underground from Cockthorne Park Station to Wood Green. Very troublesome by underground Railway, avoid it in future if possible.'

G. gandavensis

There is one final thread to the *G. gandavensis* story. Although it was seen as the Gladiolus which introduced large flowering kinds into Britain, there was another contender. William Hooker had bred a type similar in parentage some half a dozen years before Queen Victoria saw it in Paris. This was called *brenchleyensis* after Brenchley, Hooker's home town in Kent. The Reverend H. Honeywood Dombrain, in his book *The Gladiolus; its History, Cultivation and Exhibition*, wrote that he remembered buying a bulb of it in Canterbury in 1847.

Whether Sydney, Ghent or Kent had been the first horizon seen by the ancestors of the rows of summer Gladiolus Harry planted in the cut-

Above, top to bottom:
Gladiolus byzantinus,
'The Bride', 'Snow Princess'

*Right: Larkspur growing in
front of the vineries at Chilton*

flower plot, it mattered not, for they turned out to be lovely, particularly 'Snow Princess'.

If Gladiolus had been esteemed for its stately beauty, other flowers were valued in the cut-flower plot for their scent. Double Rocket (*Hesperis matronalis*), a favourite in Elizabethan times, was equally loved by Victorians. The scent is reputedly more powerful at night, hence the name *Hesperis*, but we were destined never to smell it at night or for that matter by day. It turns out that Double Rocket, thanks to a virus, has almost disappeared. It does, however, have a saviour in the form of the Hardy Plant Society. A few plants, some from Ireland, have, under the care of the Conservation Group of the society, been freed from the disease. The plants are not the white form but pale lilac, 'Lilacina Flore Pleno'. The clean-up process has taken two years and now, by virtue of micro-propagation, a few plants are available for purchase. At the time Harry was planting up his cut-flower plot, though, we could obtain only one, and that on loan. Clearly we could not cut much off this, so we turned our attention to sweetly scented Pinks and Carnations.

Of Pinks there turned out to be several old sorts still available: 'Dad's Favourite' (white with chocolate lacing); 'Earl of Essex' (rose-pink with fringed petals); 'Inchmery' (light pink); 'Sam Barlow' (white with an almost black eye) and 'Mrs Sinkins' (white). Of Carnations it was a different story, for apart from some catalogues claiming that they could offer the old 'Crimson Clove', no nineteenth-century kinds seemed to have survived. The scarcity of old varieties is nothing new. James Douglas, writing in *Hardy Florists' Flowers*, published in 1880, had noted it as well. In his day he put it down to fine old sorts having a delicate constitution and not surviving in open ground. The demise of hardy border kinds he attributed to lack of attention, meaning that they were not receiving annual propagation. It may well be that these reasons also explain the disappearance of late Victorian kinds.

Bizarre (top) and Picotee Carnations

By the mansion a Victorian gardener would probably have planted Carnations of a single colour (Selfs) for the striking effect they produced when viewed from a distance, but for the cut-flower plot, which provided flowers destined for closer scrutiny in bouquets or as buttonholes, it seemed appropriate also to have Carnations which would have been appreciated for their variation of colour. Through an act of kindness on the part of a Hampshire nurseryman, Harry acquired enough plants to form a suitably 'old-looking' selection. They included Bizarres (meaning two colours, disposed longitudinally on a white ground); Flakes (one colour laid lengthways on a white ground); Picotees (very beautiful, petals either white or yellow with a strip of colour around their edge) and Selfs (some clove-scented).

There was one group of Carnation which eluded us and had no substitute: the Malmaison. It would have been too tender for the plot outside, but a few inside the show house would have been a bonus. Malmaisons were valued for cutting in grand establishments where large flowers were wanted in plenty. Originating in France in 1857, the first ones grown in Britain had large blush-coloured blooms, similar in hue to the Rose 'Souvenir de la Malmaison'. These deluxe Carnations, sweeter in perfume than all others, had a reputation for being difficult to cultivate and were often given a house to themselves. Harry's first experience of seeing one was when his Uncle Fred dispatched him and another young gardener from the Blackmoor estate to visit and learn from Lord Horder's garden at Petersfield. Lord Horder was then, Harry believes, physician to George V. At the garden both lads were greatly impressed by a house filled with Carnations. Uncle Fred had Carnations growing in pots at Blackmoor but they had never seen any growing in beds under glass. As Harry recalls, 'We went back full of it and I can remember my Uncle saying, "Well, they weren't Carnations, boy, they were Malmaisons!"'

If Lord Horder's relatively small collection had been impressive, how grand in the late 1890s the Duchess of Portland's Malmaison houses must have been. One season they provided her with 3000 blooms. A few Malmaisons might still exist in private hands, but on the whole they're now as rare as hens' teeth.

Referring to another favoured cut flower of the era, the Sweet Pea, John Stainer Eckford said: 'Keep on cutting, keep on flowering'. He knew plenty about the subject as he was the son of Henry Eckford, the great Victorian Sweet Pea grower from Wem in Shropshire. It was through going to Wem to find out about Eckford Sweet Peas that the name of the old purple-blue Sweet Pea which Harry had grown as a backing for the herbaceous border came to light. Tom Acton, head gardener at Arley Hall in Cheshire, had kindly sent Harry a bag of seed from this Sweet Pea which he'd grown for years in the kitchen garden at Arley. He didn't know its name. Harry had sufficient left over to clothe some nut sticks set in a circle near the cut-flower plot. When this anonymous Sweet Pea bloomed, Peter Thoday, our adviser and programme presenter, had the bright idea of taking a few to Wem – not to see Henry or John Stainer Eckford, who have departed this life (their nursery is now roads and houses), but to see Val and John Good of the Eckford Sweetpea Society of Wem. Over the past few years they have formed a collection of Eckford Sweet Peas and the small, brightly coloured blooms take over a sizeable portion of their garden. It proved to be that 'our' Sweet Pea wasn't represented in the collection, but after consulting an old Eckford catalogue Val believed it to be 'Countess Cadogan', described as having a violet standard with light blue wings. Its shape definitely marked it out as Eckford-raised. Before Henry Eckford's day the standard or major petal of a Sweet Pea had little nicks or indentations in it. By breeding he succeeded in filling these out and made the standard smooth, as on 'Countess Cadogan'. He also increased the number of flowers a Sweet Pea had on each stem from two to four and made them sit more closely together on the stem than they had in former years.

Henry Eckford had begun experimenting with Sweet Peas in the 1870s when he was a head gardener in Gloucestershire. He had already had experience of improving Verbenas and Dahlias. In 1882 he raised an award-winning Sweet Pea called 'Bronze Prince' and in 1887 the first cream Sweet Pea, 'Primrose'. For many years Sweet Peas had been available in only five varieties designated by the colours black, pink, white, scarlet, and pink-and-white. Eckford's work began to add considerably to this range of colours and so many people wanted his Sweet Pea seed that he took a head gardener's job on an estate which offered him more room. It was Boreatton Park in Shropshire. However, as his new varieties and colours increased and even more seed was sought from him, he decided to leave Boreatton and set up a nursery in the nearby town of Wem. Business grew rapidly, not only in Britain but overseas as well. In America in particular there was great interest in the Sweet Pea. In the 1897 Sweet Pea catalogue of W. T. Hutchins of Indian Orchard, Massachusetts, Eckford is credited with leading the world in his work on Sweet Peas and space is given to advertise 'Eckford "novelties" for 1896'. American Sweet Peas were also introduced into Britain, and their most famous raiser, Mr W. Atlee Burpee from Philadelphia, visited Eckford at Wem. In an odd way this interchange still exists, for in Val and John Good's collection of Eckford varieties there was at the time of our visit a recent acquisition believed to be 'Cambridge Blue'. It was on the point of flowering and eagerly awaited. It had been found in America.

Among the new varieties Henry Eckford raised in 1896 was a pink Sweet Pea called 'Prima Donna'. It was the beginning of a new chapter in the history of the plant for in 1899 'Prima Donna' produced a variant which had large wavy blooms – an extraordinary sight, as all Eckford's varieties had smooth or hooded standards. This frilly novelty, as often happens in such cases, appeared simultaneously in three different places: at Althorp Park, Northampton; in Unwin's nurseries near Cambridge; and in Eckford's nursery at Wem. The sport at Cambridge, which was named 'Gladys Unwin', was small and less spectacular than the one at Althorp. The one at Wem was identical to that at Althorp. As Silas Cole,

Right top to bottom: Henry Eckford Sweet Pea, an old Eckford variety with smooth standard, a modern 'frilly' Spencer variety

Above right: Henry Eckford (left) with Mr W. Atlee Burpee

the head gardener at Althorp, had already named his 'Countess Spencer' (the Fifth Earl Spencer, ancestor of the present Princess of Wales, was Cole's employer), Henry Eckford didn't give a name to his but sold it as 'Countess Spencer'. The new wavy 'Spencer' Sweet Peas quickly overtook in popularity Eckford's other smooth-petalled varieties. Henry Eckford died in December 1905, the year in which he had raised the first orange-coloured Sweet Pea which, fittingly, bears his name.

In 1988 a Sweet Pea show was held in Wem Town Hall to celebrate Henry Eckford's centenary. It was so successful that it has become an annual event. On show day even the shop windows in the town are deco-rated with Sweet Peas. Although the majority of Sweet Peas exhibited

are modern 'Spencer' kinds, there is a special class in the show for Grandifloras, the old-fashioned pre-Spencer varieties. One part of this class acknowledges an undeniable attribute of these vintage Sweet Peas: a prize for a bowl of them judged purely for their strength of perfume.

The Dahlia had no such agreeable perfume but was valued in the Victorian cut-flower plot because it filled the void left by summer flowers which had ceased to bloom. It also, as E. S. Delamer wrote, displayed 'its finest blooms at the season when our aristocracy return from town to their country seats'.

A Mexican plant, the Dahlia had first been introduced into Britain via Madrid in 1798 but appears to have become lost. In May 1804 it was re-introduced when Mr Buonaiuti, the librarian at Holland House in London, received from Madrid seeds of three kinds sent to him by Lady Holland. One sort flowered in the gardens of Holland House in September of the same year and the other two in the following year. From these came nearly all the Dahlias grown in gardens in those early years.

The name Dahlia honoured a Swedish botanist called Dahl, but because it was so like Dalea (a genus of greenhouse herbs named after an English botanist, Dr Samuel Dale), it was suggested to change it to Georgiana after Professor Georgi, an eminent Russian traveller and botanist. In 1834 John Loudon's *Encyclopaedia of Gardening* refers to Georginas but an article written eight years later rejoices that 'public sanction' had triumphed over 'individual whim' and that the Dahlia had resisted attempts to change its name.

The first Dahlias had purple or crimson petals and single blooms but work on improving them soon got under way. In 1809 a dark red double was raised in the royal gardens at Berlin and by 1818 doubles were being grown in Britain. Dahlias were rich men's flowers; in 1835 a variety called 'Yellow Defiance' sold for £200. However, by the 1840s improvements had been carried out to such an extent and so many new sorts raised that it was rare to see a tradesman or cottager's garden without a good collection, including doubles. Depending upon the persuasion of the writers, the 1850s saw the Dahlia being described either as 'the Queen of autumnal flowers' or as a 'floral upstart' noted for its 'gaudy, flaunting' looks.

Its eye-catching appearance and the symmetry of its blooms made the Dahlia a favourite flower with which to inscribe the sovereign's name at festivals and processions. The names of some early Dahlias, though, were anything but festive: 'Metropolitan Purple' has a particularly dull ring. It was probably names which blighted Harry's enthusiasm for the Dahlia, for it is not his most favourite flower. Freud would say it went back to the days when Harry worked for Captain Thackeray at Wode

Left: Silas Cole, head gardener at Althorp Park

House. The Captain had a large 'S'-shaped lawn and on either side of it several hundred Dahlias. Harry says that there were upwards of forty different kinds and by the end of his first summer he was expected to name each without looking at the label.

But Dahlias did have a champion, for David, Harry's young assistant, loves them. Like his father he grows them for exhibition. David was charged with getting a supply of nineteenth-century kinds for the cut-flower plot. Using his 'inside' knowledge, he came up with the name of David Brown as the grower reputed to have the largest collection of Dahlias in the world. When asked, Mr Brown kindly checked his lists to see what Victorian varieties he had and brought the following to the garden: *Dahlia merckii* (a species with small purple flowers); 'White Aster' (1879, a Miniature Decorative); 'Kaiser Wilhelm' (1890, a Small Ball, the flower a blend of red, yellow and cream); and 'Tommy Keith' (1892, a Miniature Ball, bi-coloured red/white).

Dahlia 'Kaiser Wilhelm'

He also brought some 'Bishop of Llandaff', a scarlet-flowered Dahlia stunning for its rich dark foliage. Harry had expressed a liking for the 'Bishop' and, as it turned out, although it was not a Victorian variety, it was a very happy choice, because when Harry went to Tredegar House, Newport, the location chosen in which to film him decorating rooms with flowers, he met Mrs Clarice Barrett. Mrs Barrett keeps in order Tredegar's collection of glasshouses and a partially walled garden, but sixty-odd years ago she worked for Mr Fred Treseder in Cardiff. Mr Treseder had a nursery and bred Dahlias. Clarice recalls that there used to be little piles of seed lying around there which everyone had to be careful not to disturb. Such care, combined with Mr Treseder's skill, resulted in 1928 in his raising 'Bishop of Llandaff'. Mr Treseder was a kindly man and Clarice remembers that he let out plants of the 'Bishop' to various people. Unfortunately this kindness went against him, for it soon led to other nurseries raising their own stocks and doing a great trade. Clarice didn't have the 'Bishop' in her garden but Harry promised her some.

The lateness of blooming which made Dahlias sought after as cut flowers also rendered them susceptible to frost. Some Victorian garden-ers planted them in large pots which could be moved into shelter. Frost also bedevilled the 'last showy flower of the year' – the Chrysanthemum. In the 1820s there were forty-eight varieties of Chinese Chrysanthe-mum known in British gardens. They had been introduced over a span of roughly thirty-five years but, 'on account of their delicacy' not one was recommended to be grown in an open border. Instead garden manuals advised a warm spot in front of a wall or palings. The Chrysanthemums could be fan-trained on to this and it would also help support any form

Pompon Chrysanthemums

of protection placed over them on frosty nights. Although by mid-century reference is made to improved varieties sufficiently acclimatised to flower in open borders, Chrysanthemums destined as cut flowers for the mansion were grown in pots in glasshouses. This state of affairs went on until comparatively recent times, for in all the private gardens in which he has worked Harry can remember only an odd few Chrysanthemums grown outside; the rest were all under glass. At his present estate he used to have a thousand pots of them standing in the Peach houses. Few were sold; most went to supply the mansion from October to the middle of January.

A favourite Chrysanthemum in Victorian times was the Pompon, which was particularly useful for cutting as it flowered freely. It was the result of two miniature flowering varieties introduced by Robert Fortune in about 1847. One was *minimum* and the other Fortune called 'the Chusan Daisy'. The Chusan was a small semi-double, reddish-brown in colour. Both were propagated and distributed to Horticultural Society members and some found their way to France where seedlings of various colours were raised. Some of these were perfectly symmetrical and the French called these Pompons because the small compact flowers looked like the pompon on a soldier's cap. A Hammersmith nurseryman, John Salter, imported them into Britain. Pompons grown for cutting purposes were cultivated in bush form, but if trained up as standards they provided useful decoration for the dining-room table: their heads were high enough not to interrupt the diners' line of vision and they looked well under artificial light.

Pompon standard

Robert Fortune was also responsible for the arrival of Japanese Chrysanthemums, introducing seven varieties in 1861. Their shapes were viewed at first as grotesque and they were ridiculed, but they eventually found favour because of their rich colours. Some even attracted the epithet 'graceful', though this is not a word one could truthfully use to describe the globular incurved Chrysanthemums that Harry grows; 'statuesque' would be nearer the mark. Harry says his sort are now rarely seen in private gardens. They used to be valued to fill large vases and as pot plants at the foot of the mansion staircase. In the summer months, when they were still growing, he stood their pots out in a row on the terrace of the kitchen garden. At each end of the row a stake was driven into the ground and a few strands of wire tied across to support the Chrysanthemums as they went ever upwards. Some used to reach over 6 feet (1.8 m) in height. In years gone by Harry's glasshouse foreman, a man of slight build, had a pair of stepladders to help him tend them.

The poetic Victorian writer of *Days and Hours in a Garden* admires the 'delicious confusion of petals' in the giant exhibition Japanese Chrysanthemums, believing that this chaos helped the 'wonderful effect of colour'. This was not a view held by all. Edwin Molyneaux, gardener to W. H. Myers Esq. of Bishops Waltham and a doyen amongst Chrysanthemum growers, wrote a comprehensive little book published in 1886 called *Chrysanthemums and their Culture, A Practical Treatise on Propagating, Growing and Exhibiting from the Cutting to the Silver Cup*. In this Mr Molyneaux recommends gardeners providing themselves with certain appliances to manipulate Chrysanthemum flowers for, even if they were intended as home decoration, 'a few minutes attention given to a flower improves its appearance greatly'. Such appliances, preferably kept in a velvet-lined box, included a camel-hair brush for dusting and a collec-

Below: Box of appliances for 'dressing' Chrysanthemums and using the tweezers to titivate the flower

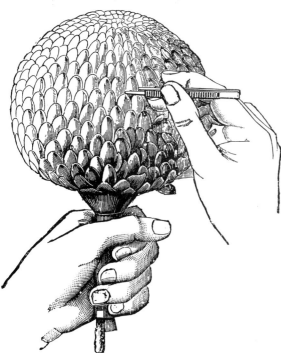

tion of different-sized tweezers for arranging the petals. The tweezers could be steel or ivory. Ivory ones cut down the risk of bruising the petals but didn't grip so well. Gardeners wishing to take advantage of the tweezers' other potential, to eradicate earwigs, were probably wise to choose steel. The insects, renowned for feeding on Chrysanthemum petals after dark, could be located by lantern light and quickly caught in the tweezers. Harry had a pair of metal tweezers which, he said, had been at the garden all of this century and had been handed down from one foreman to the next. Although he hadn't gone to the extremes of titivating Chrysanthemum flowers before they went on display in the mansion, the tweezers had been used to 'dress' those sent to flower shows.

At the turn of the century the estate's head gardener, Charles Beckett, had grown five hundred pots of large incurved Chrysanthemums for entry in competitions. The first ever competitive show for 'cut blooms' of Chrysanthemums had been held as early as 1846. Evidence that Mr Beckett did well is in the thatched fruit store in the garden at Chilton. The wall just inside the door is papered with award cards. They are black with age but an occasional enquiring finger has revealed the embossed gold medals still bright. Harry in his heyday grew three hundred exhibition Chrysanthemums and reckoned that if he got a third of them to show standard he was lucky. It was a costly and time-consuming business. The size of each flower head was roughly 8 inches (20 cm) across and the same down, and it could take up to an hour to dress it. Harry's last foreman used to spend hours with the tweezers.

In the autumn, when Harry's latest batch bloomed, he showed David how 'dressing' was done. First he found a 'bolster'. This device had been made in the days when the garden had its own carpenter who could turn his hand to such niceties. Tied to the stem when the flower head was turned upside down, the bolster had a wire ring 3 inches (7.5 cm) in diameter which fitted beneath the hanging nether petals, supporting them and bolstering them out. Turning the bloom the right way up, Harry explained that each petal in turn should be lifted by the tweezers and laid like thatch on a roof, and the top of the bloom made as flat as a cake – that is, except for a bit in the middle the size of a decapitated walnut: this was left to show that it hadn't opened and that the flower was at its peak. When Harry had finished, the bloom looked finely coiffured. In former times, together with others, it would have been fitted into a box specially made by the garden's carpenter and transported to the competition venue. The carpenter would have gone along as well, to take the nails out of the box when it reached the show.

CHAPTER TEN
Flower Shows

Flower shows – 'Specimen' plants – Exhibition problems – Florists' flowers – An Auricula theatre – How the Pansy came in from the fields – Tulips in beer bottles.

London Horticultural Society shows began in 1827. At first they met with little success, for only a few cultivators bothered to display their produce under 'a small iron tent'. However, liberal rewards proved enticing and it became a mark of distinction to win one. The popularity of the shows grew to such an extent that by 1842 the *Quarterly Review* was lauding them as having 'done wonders in improving public taste and exciting the emulation of nurserymen. It is something, even if the prize is missed, to know that your flower will be gazed at by five or six thousand critical admirers.'

A flower show at the Botanic Gardens, Regent's Park, April 1870

The *Review* believed that shows had also brought another benefit, a common scene of enjoyment, 'an orderly and happy mass, from the labourer of the soil to the queen upon the throne'. The latter gave the society her seal of approval in 1861 by granting it a new charter changing its name to the Royal Horticultural Society. In that year the society opened its gardens at South Kensington and had an exhibition to mark the occasion. An Orchid called *Laelia purpurea* (Nicholson's *Dictionary of Gardening* calls it 'one of the noblest for exhibition purposes') was, with its thirty-six full-blown blooms, the best single 'specimen' present.

The desire to exhibit 'specimens' led gardeners to produce plants of extraordinary size. It got to the point where the larger specimens had difficulty in getting through the doors of the exhibition hall! A fine example is the convex Pompon Chrysanthemum specimen illustrated in Shirley Hibberd's *The Amateur's Greenhouse and Conservatory*. In the 1860s it became noted that prizes for specimen plants always went to gardeners with glasshouses large enough to grow monstrous plants and exhibitors with only small glasshouses who could only grow 'small' specimens went unrewarded. To overcome this the president of the Lincoln Horticultural Society offered to working amateurs a garden frame for the best collection of small plants arranged in the space the frame would occupy – roughly 36 square feet (3.3 square m). The class became so successful that other shows took it up and extended it to groups of larger size. In 1875 it was adopted by the Royal Horticultural Society. These classes for groups of plants arranged for effect had a double benefit. Not only did they allow more people to compete in shows but they also brought attention to the decorative value of small plants and how one could be used to complement another.

Specimen Chrysanthemum illustrated in Shirley Hibberd's The Amateur's Greenhouse and Conservatory

In addition to being instructive, flower shows earned a reputation as 'centres of sweetness and light'. But occasionally a shadow fell across them. Henry A. Bright, in *The English Flower Garden* (1881), poses the question: 'Are the flower-shows, the number of which is constantly increasing, an advantage or not?' He then goes on to answer this himself, citing as points of argument that gardeners planning to compete in shows give undue attention to the plants which will secure them prizes; that the 'dressing' of flowers could lead to worse forms of dishonesty; and that the system of prize tickets which announce 'Mr . . . . . . gardener to . . . . . .' make the owner a nobody compared to the gardener. In short, flower shows, Mr Bright believes, are not an advantage and 'it is the wiser course for anyone who really cares about his garden, and would rather have a succession of well-cultured flowers than some merely exceptional success, to discourage his gardener from exhibiting.'

On flower shows organised by horticultural societies in the shires, other shadows fell. For those with insubstantial funds a wet show day could spell ruin. Then there was the question of the prize money they gave, often amounts so small that they failed to attract competitors. A gardener writing to the *Journal of Horticulture and Cottage Gardener* about Sherborne Flower Show in 1877, put it thus: 'Now, as the bulbs (Gladiolus) cost 5s [25p] or 7s 6d [37½p] each, it is of course not exceedingly likely that an amateur will cut his spikes and spoil his garden for the short time the Gladioli are in bloom, pay 2s 6d [12½p] entrance fee and his railway expenses, all for the chance of winning 10s [50p].'

In 1860 a curate, the Reverend S. H. Parkes, started a flower show in Bloomsbury, London. It was confined to 'the inhabitants of the narrowest and most thickly populated street in the parish and the only rule was that an exhibitor must have had his plant in his possession for three weeks. Its success led to a similar show being organised the following year, with the flowers limited this time, to help judging, to Geraniums, Fuchsias and annuals. In 1863 the show was honoured by the name the Bloomsbury Workingmen's Flower Show and Lord Shaftesbury came to give away the prizes. The first prize for adults in each class was 10s (50p) and for children 5s (25p). A woman servant did very well for she gained first prize in all three classes with the very same plants she'd won prizes with at the last show. As to the other competitors, the *Telegraph* is alleged to have written that those who seemed to know least of what was going on were the poor people themselves. There seemed to be no means of rousing them.

The above was a far cry from the enthusiasm displayed by those who cultivated and exhibited 'florists' flowers' in the Spitalfields area of London and who had their counterparts in the manufacturing towns of the Midlands and the North of England. A 'florists' flower' was one which had been raised or originated from seed in the garden of a 'florist'. The term 'florist' didn't mean, as it does today, a person who sells flowers in a shop but described an enthusiast who raised and selected certain flowers with the aim of creating them to an ideal of perfection. In the early part of the nineteenth century the Auricula, Polyanthus, Tulip, Carnation, Pink, Ranunculus, Anemone and Hyacinth were all florists' flowers. As in the case of the Gooseberry shows which are still held in Cheshire, the venue for showing was often a local public house.

Overleaf: Florists' flowers (left) and the Auricula stand at Calke Abbey (right)

During the years leading up to the middle part of the century florists' flowers declined in numbers. The fashion for brightly coloured bedding plants ousted the old English florist's Tulips, and space formerly given in glasshouses to Carnations was taken over by the bedding plants which had to be over-wintered in their thousands. Other florists' flowers which had never found a home in fashionable gardens owed their decline to the fact that many of the small gardens in which they had once been cultivated disappeared under bricks and mortar. In the 1860s there appears to have been a revival of interest and a determination by florists to be noticed, reflected in the words of a correspondent to the *Journal of*

SUTTON'S STRAINS OF FLORIST'S FLOWERS.

Double Portulaca.
Cineraria.
Dianthus.
Calceolaria.
Giant Cyclamen.

SUTTON & SONS,
THE QUEEN'S SEEDSMEN, READING.

Horticulture and Cottage Gardener: 'We poor florists have been so thrust aside by whipper-snappers, like "Tom Thumb", yellow Calceolarias, variegated mint! and everything that can be pressed into the bedding line, that we must stand up for ourselves, or we shall be overwhelmed.'

An opportunity for standing up presented itself at the increasingly popular flower shows being held around the country. In the year 1861 an Auricula enthusiast wrote: 'There has not been for many years – not, I should think, since the gathering at the Horns Tavern, Kennington, when John Dickson was king of growers – so large a display of Auriculas seen in London as at the April show at the Royal Botanic Gardens.' There is other evidence of the Auricula finding fresh favour too. In 1863 ladies stopping to admire them at flower shows apparently obstructed the thoroughfare with their distended garments, and demand for plants made it impossible to obtain ones of any size.

Charles Turner, a nurseryman from Slough, was the chief supplier in the South of England. Turner also bred new sorts of Alpine Auricula and helped popularise them. These, with their bright colours and yellow centres, were recommended as good starting plants for those about to take up Auricula growing. They were easier to cultivate than the 'shows' or 'fancies'. These had been literally bred for shows, and a great part of their attraction lay in the ring of 'paste' in the centre of each flower and white powdery 'meal' which, on some, covered the flowers, leaves and stems. To avoid this paste and meal being washed off by rain, show Auriculas had to be (and still are) grown in garden frames and glasshouses. Victorian manuals advised great care in watering them and, to stop accidental drops falling on to the crown or foliage, recommended a small watering pot with a spout 1 foot 6 inches (45 cm) long, bent at the end and then contracted to the diameter of a goose quill. For diet they advised not the old florists' juicy pieces of raw meat, but a rich compost consisting of rotted cow manure, leaf mould and turfy loam.

The neat and beautiful blooms of Auriculas could provide their Victorian cultivators with quite personal 'shows'. When they were on the point of blooming their removal was recommended from glasshouse or frame to another structure which still afforded protection but also enabled the flowers to be seen and admired. The *Journal of Horticulture and Cottage Gardener* for 5 May 1863 illustrates an 'Auricula-house for blooming'. This, 7 feet (2 m) in height, appears to have boarding from ground level to half-way up. From that point the sides and the roof are of glass. There are five shelves inside graduating in height, the bottom one at 3 feet 6 inches (1 m) above ground level, and the idea being that 'placed on a level with the sight, the plants can be seen without the trouble of stooping over them'. The glass sashes in the front could be drawn up to allow air inside.

Loudon's *Encyclopaedia of Gardening*, of some thirty years earlier, illustrates an Auricula 'Blooming stage' which, although in some respects is cruder than the one described above, has curious touches of refinement. For example, the inside of the back, the sides and the graduated shelves were all to be painted black or some other dark colour 'by way of contrast to the white eyes &c., of the flowers'. It was also possible, by positioning a mirror at either end, to make the Auriculas placed on its shelves appear to stretch into infinity.

At Calke Abbey in Derbyshire (now owned by the National Trust) there is a structure in a corner of the gardens. When it was made by the estate carpenter in 1857 it was called a 'verandah' but by 1880 it is recorded as being 'a stand for Auriculas'. It is unusual to find an Auricula stand at such grand gardens. Indeed, *Flora Domestica* writing of Auriculas in 1823 says:

> A fine stage of these plants is scarcely ever to be seen in the gardens of the nobility and gentry, who depend upon the exertions of hired servants and cannot therefore compete in these nicer operations of gardening with those who tend their flowers themselves, and watch over their progress with paternal solicitude.

Hollyhock

In 1880 James Douglas, head gardener at Loxford Hall, Ilford, Essex, published a book called *Hardy Florists' Flowers*. Douglas, one of a band of men who had helped revive interest in the Auricula, was often approached by amateurs who were interested in growing florists' flowers but were unable to find any written information on the subject. Reflecting on this, he decided to write the book to meet what he believed was a 'growing want'. By this time the term florists' flower encompassed more than the Auricula, Tulip, Pink and so on of the early part of the century. Douglas' book includes chapters on the Chrysanthemum, Dahlia, Gladiolus, Hollyhock, Phlox, Aquilegia and Pansy. Of these, the earliest 'new' recruit had been the Pansy. Florists turned their attention to the flower in the 1830s.

The Pansy's rise to notice is worth outlining for, unlike many florists' flowers, it originated not in some exotic foreign country but in the cornfields of England. As a small wild flower it had long been a favourite, affectionately known by a variety of names: Heartsease, Love-in-Idleness, Call-me-to-you and Herb trinity (a reference to the three colours it often displayed in one bloom). Until about 1813 it remained unaltered, then Lady Bennett, daughter of the Earl of Tankerville, asked her gardener, William Richardson, to grow and improve some wild

Pansies (*Viola tricolor*) in her garden at Walton-on-Thames. James Lee, a Hammersmith nurseryman, saw the results of Richardson's efforts and encouraged him to continue hybridising and selecting. At the same time, at Iver in Buckinghamshire, Lord Gambier collected in the fields near his mansion some wild yellow-and-white Pansies (*Viola lutea*) and, taking them to his gardener, William Thomson, asked him to cultivate them in the garden. Thomson integrated into his crosses another species, the first true blue Viola which he obtained from a nurseryman in Slough. Simultaneously, at Lady Bennett's garden, William Richardson also worked with a similar blue-flowered plant but obtained his from James Lee.

At this point it appears that Mr Thomson, Lord Gambier's gardener, takes up the running, for among the many seedlings he raised were several fine enough to merit names. One of these was called 'Thomson's King', and its creator considered it to be 'the first good-shaped flower'. None of the improved Pansies had the blotch now so familiar on Pansy faces; instead they had a few dark lines. A one-time neighbour of Mr Thomson talked over with him the appearance of the first blotched Pansy and later recorded Thomson's account of how the event occurred: 'It was entirely the offspring of chance. On looking one morning over a collection of Heaths which had been sadly neglected, I was struck (to use a vulgar expression), all of a heap, by seeing what appeared to me a miniature impression of a cat's face steadfastly gazing at me.' The 'cat's face' was on the bloom of a self-sown Pansy and was the result of the usual dark lines having fused into a blotch. Thomson called the seedling 'Madora' and from it came other blotched varieties. In fact he went on to raise so many that he was forced to consult his book of Shakespeare to find enough names!

Florists continued improvements to the Pansy and for their shows strove for a bloom which was round in outline, flat and smooth at the edge, and with a dense circular blotch. In the 1850s these 'show' Pansies gradually became joined by 'Fancy' types. They were imported from France or Belgium and, in an odd way, were coming home, for they owed their origin to the first blotched Pansies. They were first offered for sale by John Salter of Versailles Nursery, London. Florists thought them small and badly shaped but found their markings interesting and curious and set to work to improve them. There appeared in Scotland a larger, brighter strain which also had the merit of being more vigorous than the continental type. Unlike 'show' Pansies their stems didn't have to be thinned out to encourage good blooms; the more flowers they carried, the better the flowers appeared to be. It was this trait which led to speculation that fancy Pansies would make good bedding plants, but in the

Right: Show Pansy

Far right: Fancy Pansy

Below right: English florists' Tulips

main they remained as exhibition flowers. Bedding 'Violas' were to come from crossing both show and fancy types with wild species.

Some half a dozen beautiful blowsy varieties of fancy Pansies are still offered by specialist nurseries, as are an even smaller number of neat, circular-faced show Pansies. Those who have seen both will appreciate the view of one late Victorian writer who, on charting the rise of bedding Violas, ends by remarking: 'To the florist, however, a show-board of "show" or "fancy" Pansies gives the keenest pleasure, and the delight with which he examines a bed of choice varieties is unbounded.'

Not with the intention of 'showing', but for their beauty and interest, Harry had a small patch of these old sorts of Pansies. Their bed was in the north border of the kitchen garden. The sun, making its way across the sky, left this border in shadow from ten in the morning, and on hot summer days old farmyard manure and leaf mould worked into the soil helped keep their roots damp.

At the opposite end of the garden, to catch the early spring warmth which reflected from the south-facing wall, he had a small patch of English florists' Tulips. They had to be kept at a distance from any Lilies, for unfortunately the virus which is responsible for the Tulips' beautiful flamed and feathered markings is anathema to Lilies. It has been said that Tulip enthusiasts who used to exhibit these old sorts at general horticultural shows were viewed with suspicion by Lily breeders showing their wares in the near vicinity. In Wakefield each year there is no such embarrassment, for at the Wakefield and North of England Tulip Society Show only Tulips are exhibited. The old florists' Tulip is no longer commercially available and is kept in existence by the enthusiasm of a small band of society members. Years ago each Tulip was exhibited in a special glazed conical pot, but these are now rarer than the Tulips and instead members use rich brown beer bottles. It is an interesting remnant of the old florists' flower shows, for the Tulips are judged to the standards and by rules laid down 150 years ago.

CHAPTER ELEVEN
Forcing Flowers

Forcing bulbs – Summer 'plunge' beds – The fashion for Lilac –
Venus in a rage – Cape Heaths – A very early spring.

The frail image of Mr Beckett's herbaceous border, *circa* 1900, which hangs in the window of Harry's office, has a companion of those times – a head gardener's produce book. The book may, in fact, have inhabited the office for more years than the picture but, afforded the protection of closed pages, it is more decipherable. It lists in daily columns the amounts of fruit and vegetables which were sent to the mansion.

Snowdrops

Among the mushrooms, Brussels sprouts and seakale of the winter months are records of sprays of Orchids, bunches of Violets, Lilac, Roman Hyacinths, Daffodils, Tulips, Aconites, Chionodoxa, Snowdrops and other flowering bulbs. As it would have been too early in the year for many of these flowers to bloom naturally, it is obvious that, apart from the Snowdrops, they would have been forced. Snowdrops, according to Harry, do not force well. He forwards them by about ten or twelve days by simply digging up a clump from the vast patches near the fruit house, potting it and putting it into a warm glasshouse. He also still forces a few Hyacinths and Narcissus, particularly large bowls of 'Paperwhite', but not to the extent he did years ago. However, adopting his role of 'Victorian' head gardener, he said that he would, as near as possible, force a collection of bulbs which wouldn't have looked out of place in the garden a hundred years ago.

The task of finding Victorian varieties of Daffodil bulbs was simple. Beneath the turf of the small orchard by the kitchen garden were the old, slender, gap-petalled varieties described earlier. In the summer, after their foliage had died down, Harry lifted a selection and put them to dry preparatory to potting. Added to them were some specially purchased: *Narcissus obvallaris* (the true Tenby Daffodil); *N. poeticus albus plenus odoratus*; *N. bulbocodium*; 'Paperwhite Snowflake' (1895); and 'King Alfred' (1899).

As regards Hyacinths and Tulips there was quite formidable advice in the *Cottage Gardener and Country Gentleman* (August 1860 edition), which

recommended: 'If you wish a score of Hyacinths in bloom on Christmas Day, and as many pots of early Tulips, you would require to have at least three score pots of each to choose from.' Sixty Tulips and sixty Hyacinths seemed a little excessive, and as we didn't have to meet that particular festive deadline Harry opted for six of the dozen or so Victorian varieties of Hyacinth and Tulip still available.

For early forcing Hyacinths he selected the following varieties: 'Bismarck' (mid-violet, 1875); 'L'Innocence' (ivory-white, 1863); and 'La Victoire' (light carmine, 1875). Late forcers chosen were: 'Lady Derby' (rose pink, 1875); 'Lord Balfour' (wine coloured-violet, 1883); and 'Distinction' (outside maroon, inside beetroot-purple, 1880). 'Distinction' might sound rather dull but when it flowered it was extraordinary, not the least for its red/maroon stem.

Tulips included: 'Duc Van Thol' (red and yellow, 1750); 'Peach Blossom' (a very lovely double early, whose pinkish green-edged flower when opened out fully was as wide as a teacup, 1890). Selected not for their forcing ability but because they are interesting species were: *batalinii* (very pale creamy yellow, no exact date for this); *T. saxatilis* (rosy lilac with yellow base, 1827); *T. tarda* (white with yellow base, outside brownish-purple, 1890); and *T. sprengeri* (scarlet with olive base, 1894).

The bulb order swelled with the inclusion of some old varieties of Grape Hyacinth, and Crocus of every colour but yellow, which does not force well.

Harry potted all the bulbs in late August. Years ago, in addition to pots, he said he also planted up old kipper boxes; in the case of Tulips it was twenty-four bulbs to a box. Their inelegant base hadn't mattered as they went to the mansion as cut flowers. At this point there was an unexpected hitch in the bulb-forcing operation – lack of cinder ash. The chief provider of this useful commodity, the stoke hole of the garden heating boiler, had ceased its supply years ago. The ash was needed to make a plunge bed in which the potted-up bulbs could be placed and make plenty of roots which would equip them for the rigours of forcing. Nowadays Harry makes his plunge beds out of beech leaves, but he was anxious to show how it was done in the old days. The lack of ash turned out to be temporary, for Harry managed to acquire several bucketfuls. I can only think that passers-by in those hot August days must have decided it was heat haze coming from his cottage chimney! Fortunately the bottom of the garden frame in which the pots were to be placed was covered with a layer of cinder ash left from years ago. Harry put the pots into the frame 'pot thick', as he called it – that is, almost interlocking. When all were in place they were watered and the water left to drain

Left: Forced bulbs bring an early spring to Chilton

from their surfaces. Cinder ash was then sprinkled over until it filled every crevice and eventually formed a layer over the pots to a depth of 6 inches (15 cm).

Advice on forcing bulbs seemed to vary from one Victorian manual to another. Some recommended potting up bulbs at different times between August and October in order to achieve succession; others advised potting all the bulbs up at once, plunging them and then taking only the most forward to the forcing pit. Harry believed in the latter method. He said that simply by marking the place in the plunge bed which held the early varieties, he could go straight to them and lift them without disturbing others.

The first check on progress was to be made in November and if, by that time, the early Hyacinths had made plenty of good roots and had put up a shoot the size of Harry's thumb, they would be put into a cold greenhouse to green up. The next stage would be to give them heat gradually. If it were added too quickly there was a risk that the leaves wouldn't form properly and the flower spikes would become distorted. In the past, when Harry had had to get vast quantities of early varieties out of a plunge bed at the same time, he said they could be coped with by putting some into a cold frame with 'air left on'. These would tick over happily until the time came for them to go into heat.

The old produce book with its record of the bunches of flowers cut from forced bulbs and sent to the mansion at Chilton told only half the story, for many pots of forced bulbs would also have been required to decorate the garden's show house. Alongside them would have been stood other forced flowers, including no doubt pots of *Dicentra spectabilis*, a Victorian favourite which Robert Fortune had introduced from China in 1846. E. S. Delamer wrote that it 'alone was well worth the journey thither'. Victorian books refer to it as 'Dielytra' but it still retains its other old name, Bleeding Heart, a reference to its pink heart-shaped flowers. Clumps could be kept in a reserve garden and lifted into heat successively from February until they flowered naturally outside.

Dicentra would probably have been accompanied by pots of another pretty perennial which responded well to forcing, Solomon's Seal. Crowns or pips as the individual buds were known of Lily-of-the-Valley, too, might have stood on the show house staging. Harry still has the wire cones once used to display these sweet-smelling flowers. The cones were filled tightly with moss and forcing pips of Lily-of-the-Valley eased into the moss with a small wooden dibber. When it bloomed the plant, taking its shape from the hidden wire, stood in pyramids of white blossom. Above the Lily-of-the-Valley and as sweetly scented might well have been tendrils of forced wild Honeysuckle. Plants dug out of hedgerows could be made to bloom from Christmas onwards. At Christmas, too, there might have been Pompon Chrysanthemums, their out-of-season appearance gained by placing their pots behind a north wall in October, and, for the New Year, rows of Christmas Roses, not forced but potted and taken into a glasshouse in late September and encouraged to produce blooms of 3 inches (7.5 cm) in diameter.

Not mentioned in old books but done, Harry says, in his day was the cutting of branches from outside bushes of Forsythia and Rhododendron. Placed in a warm glasshouse for a few days these would blossom and provide a useful splash of colour in a conservatory in early winter. By late winter and early spring large pot grown Rhododendrons could be brought into early flower; not only these but Azalea, Genista, Deutzia, Camellia, flowering Cherries and Lilac too (the latter also useful as cut flowers). During the hot days of summer these flowering shrubs would have stood in a 'summer plunge bed'. When Harry first came to Chilton there was such a plunge bed in a patch of ground on the east side of the thatched fruit house. He says it was as big in area as the floor of the fruit house, approximately 20 × 12 feet (6 × 3.6 m), and dug out to a depth of 9 inches (23 cm). It was filled in with leaf mould so old and fine that it was almost like ordinary soil. Each year more was added and through the summer months the pots were plunged in it up to their rims. It was also an ideal cool spot for the Lilies, which were being flowered in succession. The composition of the bed meant that it held moisture, so the pots didn't have to be watered as frequently as ones standing out in the open garden. Being in the shadow of the fruit house, the bed was cool too. From early winter, after the first frosts had chilled them, the pots of shrubs were lifted out in succession and brought into a warm glasshouse to encourage them to bloom out of season. Harry recalls having the Fig house floor covered with plants of *Azalea indica* each a yard across!

If large quantities of Lilac were to be forced for *cut* flowers they may have been grown in rows in the kitchen garden. According to an account written on Lilac forcing in 1877, gardeners of that time would also have boosted supplies from their shrubbery borders. Inspection of the borders in the autumn could reveal clumps of Lilac which needed thinning and, in these, plants with prominent buds were selected and partially cut round. Throughout the winter they could be lifted as and when needed for forcing. There obviously was a need, for Victorian journals contain many eulogies to forced Lilac, some noting that there is no other flower so deliciously fragrant during mid-winter and that just two or three sprays can perfume the whole air of a room for days.

It also seems that the whiter the blooms, the more they were valued as cut flowers. Owing to its pure whiteness a favourite Victorian variety was 'Charles X'. In fact this Lilac, if allowed to flower normally, had a dark flower, but forcing rendered it white and, because it was more vigorous than pale varieties, its foliage also tended to be stronger and less yellow-green. Why forcing turned Lilac bloom white no one really knew and as late as 1928 a monograph records it as a subject for much discussion: was it, for instance, the high temperature, or the air of the forcing house, or perhaps that Lilac was forced in darkness? There appeared to be no conclusive answer. It worried not Victorian gardeners who knew that if they put pots of Lilac in a darkened stoke hole, or in a warm dark mushroom house, after three weeks they could cut a basketful of fragrant white blooms. Having made much of white Lilac, it is only fair to say that in the 1890s there was a fashion for forced *coloured* Lilac; but perhaps because it was more difficult to obtain, in that it had to be done with less heat and much more slowly than normal, the fashion was brief. For those bold enough to cheat a paper written in 1893 lists various pigments as recommended by the Société Nationale d'Agriculture (no doubt intended for France's thriving Lilac industry). If these were dissolved in water and the stems of ordinary forced white Lilac put into the water, the blooms would take up the colour: azure, salmon-pink, orange-yellow or carmine!

For anyone contemplating forcing Lilac today it might be worthwhile reverting to the Victorian practice of getting your plant from an established clump. It is extremely difficult to obtain plants with sufficient flower buds for forcing from a British nursery. Apparently only in Holland, where Lilac is sold as part of the cut-flower trade, it is still felt worth the expense of forcing a plant then resting it for three years, as is necessary for satisfactory results.

When Cupid reckoned that some girls out-did Venus in sweetness, she, in an unladylike rage, beat them black and blue. The descendants of these poor unfortunate girls regularly went, according to the Chilton Produce book, in bunches to the mansion – for they were Violets. Through the months from December to February, Harry says, they would have been forced. Forcing Violets began early; to ensure that there would be sufficient supplies, cuttings were taken in April. Harry recalls that when he was at Stansted Park it was the responsibility of the pleasure ground men to plant these cuttings out in a cool spot and through the summer keep them sprayed with soot water to discourage red spider. Some time towards the middle of August the young plants were lifted and put into frames in a bed of leaf mould and coarse sand. On sunny winter mornings, when the Violets were in bloom, the frame tops had to be lifted to allow air in. Harry remembers that the scent

Right: Harry examines the blooms on a forced Lilac

Far right: Hyacinth 'Distinction'

Below right: Dicentra spectabilis (alias Bleeding Heart)

which poured out used to follow him right back up to the top of the frame yard.

When he came to Chilton, Harry grew four frames of forced Violets for the lady of the house. The frames in the kitchen garden had the luxury of hot-water pipes to keep out the frost. At Ashburnham Place, where Harry had been a journeyman, the system had been more interestingly archaic. He used to help make up faggots of brushwood which were laid on the ground to the length and width of a frame base – approximately 6 × 3 feet (1.8 × 1 m). On top of the faggots was tipped a layer of dried leaves whose purpose was to stop the top bit of the 'sandwich', the mixture of leaf mould and sand, placed in a frame base, from filtering down through the brushwood. When the Violets were planted, a glazed top or 'light' was put on to the frame. Although it was not heated, Harry says that the brushwood base helped distance the bed from the cold ground. On very cold nights the top was covered with matting. Harry made up a bed on the same lines for the Parma Violets he still has in his garden. It was not based on faggots of brushwood but on springy bundles of stems which David had just pruned out of a row of blackcurrants. They were, if anything, more comfortable for the 'bruised girls'.

During its hottest months the temperature on the upland of the Cape of Good Hope averages only 4°F (2°C) higher than 'that of July near London'. This useful snippet, which appeared in *The Gardener's Assistant* (1859 edition), illustrates that Cape Heaths should not receive too much heat. Indeed, it says somewhat mysteriously that their house should be built north to south so that the sun falls on them obliquely instead of perpendicularly, and their pots should be placed in rows north to south

Left to right: Making a Violet bed. 1 Putting a layer of dried leaves onto bundles of blackcurrant prunings. 2 The frame base goes on top over a thin layer of leaf mould and sand. 3 After topping up with more leaf mould and sand, the frame is planted up with Violets. 4 The Violet plants in flower

so that each shades the pot behind. In *The Forcing Garden*, a useful book
for those wishing to build any structure from a Dwarf Bean house to a
Lily-of-the-Valley pit, there is a whole chapter devoted to Heath houses.
Its author, Samuel Wood, is unstinting in his appreciation of the Heaths.
For him there was 'no class of plants capable of assuming such symmetrical and elegant proportions as this, combining with the most beautiful
inflorescence, and in such abundance'.

My edition of *The Forcing Garden* was published in 1881 and it is interesting to see that at this date there was still such enthusiasm for Cape
Heaths. Their heyday had been at the end of the eighteenth century and
the beginning of the nineteenth following their collection from the
mountains above the Cape of Good Hope. However, when other new
exotic plants began to arrive in Britain, Cape Heaths became less popular. They had also attracted the reputation of being difficult to cultivate
and great emphasis was put on growing them in the right sort of peat.
This could come from Wimbledon Common or, better still, Epping
Forest where sacks could be bought for a few shillings. Their redeeming
feature was that many flowered in winter.

Without the aid of a Heath house or peat from Epping, Harry managed to produce several beautiful white-blossomed Cape Heaths to add
to the display of flowering bulbs in the show house – not that there was
much room left to display them, for the plunge beds and forcing pits
yielded a regular succession of Hyacinths, Daffodils and Tulips. Some of
the Hyacinths might have looked, as Harry put it, 'a bit Bluebell-y' but
their scent was heady, and if Tulips were 'the very perfume of the sun',
then not only had spring been made to arrive extraordinarily early, it was
also very sunny.

CHAPTER TWELVE
Mr Lee's Violets

Mr Lee's 'Victoria Regina' – How his nursery was rediscovered.

If, in the 1880s, you just couldn't think where to spend an early spring holiday, you might have consulted *The Best of Everything* for inspiration. This book, with its 1800 useful articles on how to obtain the best of everything, would not have let you down. It lists the names of two dozen suitable seaside resorts with their attractions. Should you have chosen 'Clevedon – A pleasant watering-place in Somersetshire' with 'beautiful villas embowered in trees', you would have experienced an additional benefit not mentioned in the book: the smell at Clevedon railway station. It was not unpleasant, unless you were allergic to Violets, for they were the perpetrators of this olfactory phenomenon – many, many bunches of them, their perfume creeping out of the railway parcels office, as the local paper put it in 1883, 'to the astonishment of strangers'. The flowers, destined for all parts of the country, were known locally as 'Clevedon Violets', but they had a more formal name, 'Victoria Regina'. It had been given to them by George Lee who for many years had a Violet nursery on a south-facing slope overlooking the Clevedon-to-Bristol road.

'Victoria Regina' owed its origins not to the delicate Neapolitan Violets forced in the gardens of the wealthy, but to the hardier Russian variety, introduced from Russia in about 1820. This flowered in autumn and spring in the open ground and also during winter if the weather was mild. In July 1863 the *Journal of Horticulture and Cottage Gardener* called the plant 'perhaps the most popular of all Violets' and noted that 'some improved varieties of this have from time to time appeared, an extensive grower in the West of England having issued some new varieties of it'. The grower referred to was not George Lee but a Mr Shackwell of Locksbrook Nursery, near Bristol. In about 1848 he raised a large-flowered seedling from a Russian Violet which he called 'Russian Superb'. This, plus two other similar large-flowered seedlings which were called 'Devoniensis' and 'The Giant', were all popular in the 1850s. In 1863 a nurseryman from Cranford, F. J. Graham, toppled their popularity by producing a Russian Violet similar to 'Devoniensis' and 'Russian Superb' but superior to both. He called it 'The Czar'.

George Lee's part in the Russian Violet story happened in 1871. The tale goes that, one Sunday in December of that year, he stopped off at his nursery on the way home from church. Apparently still in a religious frame of mind, he knelt down on a rock and closed his eyes to pray. When he opened them again he saw among a patch of strawberries a striking-looking Violet. It was, he thought, a seedling from a cross between two plants growing nearby, 'The Czar' and 'Devoniensis'. According to an account he gave later, Lee believed that pollination had been carried out by a bee or other insect and that the resultant seed had been brought by a mouse to the spot where he first saw it flowering. He called the seedling 'Victoria Regina' and another slightly different seedling growing alongside it 'Prince Consort' and set to work to improve both.

By 1874 Lee was writing: 'I gather from my present experience that there will be a great demand for these flowers in the larger cities and towns of the United Kingdom. They have only to be known to be appreciated. Even the working classes give them the preference at an advanced price.' The words were prophetic, at least for 'Victoria Regina', for two years later garden journals were describing it as being more robust, earlier and having larger and deeper-coloured flowers than 'The Czar'. It was also preferred to all other Violets in London's Covent Garden.

By the end of the nineteenth century the amount of 'Victoria Regina' (alias the Clevedon Violet) being dispatched from Clevedon station had dwindled. People wanted instead new varieties raised in France. These, by virtue of cross-breeding, had become distanced from Russian Violets. The most notable, 'The Princess of Wales', raised by Armand Millet in about 1889, is still available today. The Clevedon Violet still exists too, but in a confusing way. Many local people claim to have a few plants in their garden but often these differ from one garden to the next and some look suspiciously like 'The Czar'. Indeed, the true 'Victoria Regina' appeared to have gone forever until one day in 1987. Its reappearance came through the curiosity and tenacity of Jean Burrows.

In 1986 Jean wrote a history of the market gardens which were once around Tickenham, just outside Clevedon. She became intrigued when some villagers told her how members of their family had years ago worked on a nursery on a warm south-facing slope overlooking the village. Her interest deepened when she discovered that in the garden of a house on the slope many coloured Violets bloomed each winter. Violets also appeared on other pieces of land on the hillside. Jean knew that she

Previous pages: The only known photograph of George Lee. In this family group he stands in the back row fourth from the left.
Inset: 'Victoria Regina'

Below: Jean Burrows in the patch containing rows of Violets gathered from the site of Lee's nursery

had found George Lee's Violet nursery and, with the support of the various land owners, began to try to identify the Violets. Despite the passage of years, the site had been relatively undisturbed and Violet clumps live a very long time so she believed that many might still be Mr Lee's varieties.

Jean dug out a large square patch of ground and, lifting the centre plant from each distinct clump that she found, set it into the patch. The Violets were identified with a number prefaced by the initial letter of the name of the owner of the land on which they had been discovered. When they bloomed she made a drawing of each and noted the colours. Having them grown side by side helped highlight differences. The number of different Violets collected and noted soon became upwards of a hundred! Jean realised that she was working from trial grounds recorded as having existed in 1878 and in which Lee grew six hundred new varieties, each claiming 'Victoria Regina' as the parent.

On 21 March 1987 (George Lee's 170th birthday), Jean invited a group of Violet experts to look at the Violets growing in their original sites on the hillside. Three experts independently identified 'Victoria Regina'.

As to the bed of unidentified Violets taken from Lee's overgrown trial grounds, five varieties have been micro-propagated and will be sold in 1992. They will be released by the National Council for Conservation of Plants and Gardens. One bears the name 'George Lee' (there are suspicions that this may have been the variety he called 'Prince Consort' and the other four have each been given the name of a member of the Lee family.

With tenacity and obvious affection, Jean Burrows has finished, in part, work begun on Russian Violets some 120 years ago.

CHAPTER THIRTEEN
Personal Adornment

Buttonholes – Flowers for ladies' hair and dresses – Bouquets for ballroom, presentation and weddings – 'Dos' and 'Don'ts' of bouquets – Bouquet holders including one for a chaperone – 'The Language of Flowers' – Wedding flowers.

When the violet 'Victoria Regina' made its first appearance (before its twentieth-century re-emergence described in Chapter 12) it couldn't have chosen a better time. It coincided with a practice *Domestic Floriculture* (1874) described as 'becoming very fashionable' – the wearing of buttonhole bouquets and coat-flowers. The satisfaction a young clerk felt fastening a penny bunch of Violets into his buttonhole on a London street can hardly have been less than that felt by the country gentleman who, in the knowledge that nothing looked better on 'the scarlet of Nimrod's devotees', fixed Violets to his hunting coat.

The Victorian buttonhole bouquet was different from the coat-flower: the former was a small bunch of flowers, the latter a single flower. If Violets didn't please in spring, London street sellers offered other combinations for buttonhole bouquets. These included a Tea Rose surrounded by Forget-me-Nots or white Hyacinth flowers backed by blue *Scilla sibirica*. For coat-flowers the choice included single Gardenias backed by their own foliage, a small Orchid or a Tea Rosebud. In mid-summer (according to an account written in 1879) flower sellers sold Moss Roses, ready-wired for fixing to coats, 'at nearly every corner of the streets of London'. They were not the Common Moss but a stronger deep-red kind. Nurserymen found them an accommodating crop because they could be grown under orchard trees.

Mansion owners expected their gardeners to know how to make up buttonhole bouquets and, to help them, instructions under the heading 'Personal Decorations' appeared in garden manuals. Occasionally weekly journals would provide useful snippets of advice. In an 1878 edition of *The Garden*, 'Céline Forestier' (soft primrose) and 'Boule de Neige' (pure white) are recommended as buttonhole Roses, not only for their size and fragrance but for their 'staying power' too. The latter quality was also possessed by Carnations which were known to stand the heat of crowded rooms better than most flowers. Harry has a tale which illus-

Left: Flowers in a fashion plate of 1870

trates the staying power of Carnations. He is too diplomatic to say at which estate this happened, but recalls that each morning when the owners were in residence the head journeyman had to take a red Carnation to the mansion. The Carnation went together with an extract from the weather conditions book (there is no obvious connection but it is an interesting fact). If the gentleman appeared during the day it was noted by the gardeners that he always wore the Carnation in his buttonhole. At night when the young gardeners, the footmen and the housemaids waited to board the estate bus which obligingly took them to village dances, the Carnation re-appeared, but this time in the buttonhole of the gentleman's valet. Harry remembers that it used to amuse the gardeners.

The staying power of all coat-flowers could be multiplied if the wearer equipped himself with a set of slender glass tubes in various sizes. One shilling (5p) in the 1870s could purchase a dozen tubes. A tube of a size appropriate to the stem of the flower destined to be worn could, if filled with water and slipped into a tailored pocket underneath the coat collar, keep the flower fresh for hours.

The same sort of tube could also be concealed in a lady's hair to keep fresh a single flower or perhaps a spray of Orchids on a single stem. A single Camellia might be kept moist by a piece of damp cotton wool the size of a half-crown piece (slightly larger than today's 10p piece) being placed into another piece of cotton wool the size of the Camellia and the two being drawn up with wire tightly beneath the bloom. The larger piece of cotton wool acted as a base on which to put liberal dabbings of isinglass. This would stick the outer Camellia petals down on to it so that if, as often happened with Camellias, the petals began to drop off, at least the ones stuck down would remain in place!

The stamina of more complicated kinds of floral headdress relied on their maker, often the gardener. It was his job to make sure that the flowers he used weren't over-blown. It helped, too, if they were the sort that had substantial petals. Roses, Hyacinths and Lilies in general fell into this category. There was one final precaution a gardener could take to ensure that his handiwork didn't wilt and let him and the lady wearer down. *The Gardener's Assistant* (1859) advised 'impressing upon the lady's-maid that the floral head-dress must be the very last ornament to be fixed on, and that the longer it can be kept in its box, the better will it look at the end of the evening'.

Fashions in floral headdresses were inevitably dictated by fashions in hairstyle. During the early part of Victoria's reign most women wore their hair flat and smooth on top with a central parting, a bun at the back and perhaps braided sides. A wreath of flowers encircling the head looked well with this style. The front of the wreath was the widest and most imposing part, and the two sides tapered to meet at the back of the head. The art in wreath making was to keep the arrangement light. A mixture of too many flowers tended to look clumsy. The *Journal of Horti-culture and Cottage Gardener* of 28 May 1861 suggests a wreath made of red and white Hawthorn blossoms. These were to be gathered with the morning dew upon them cut off in 3-inch (7.5-cm) heads, and set aside in water while two stems of Periwinkle were cut and their bark slit to extract the pith inside. The stalks of the blossom could then be laid inside the Periwinkle stems (this sounds a very fiddly task but it was claimed that it helped to keep the blossom fresh). Beginning at one end and working towards the centre it is said that at intervals between the white, a single spray of red does 'look very lovely mounted on the bine'. A tiny piece of Larch was also to be added.

From the 1860s onwards it became fashionable to have more elaborate hairstyles. There was great use of false pieces of hair which added height and could be turned into ringlets which could either fall down the back or lie over the shoulder. Flowers worn as a coronet (on top in front) or as a spray, which if it hung below the ear was called a 'droop', suited this style. It was also fashionable to pin small flowers on to a light trail of foliage wound into the hair which fell at the back of the head.

Ladies' 'floral decoration' was not confined to their hair. It could manifest itself in shoulder sprays, some of which were like glorified gentlemen's buttonholes, others long and curving. Then there were

Left: Camellias

Right: The Opera Box *by Henry O'Neil (1817–1880)*

garlands designed to be pinned around the dress. Like wreaths for the hair, dress-garlands needed, according to *The Garden* (7 March 1874), practice 'to make them nice and light-looking'. Their foundation was a long piece of wire and each flower was bound on to it with plenty of damp moss wound round the flower stem. Bouvardia and Stephanotis looked light and elegant, and sprays of Ivy, Japanese Honeysuckle or Creeping Myrtle could be interwoven among the flowers.

Finally, and most important, was a lady's bouquet. Like floral headdresses, the bouquet went through stages of fashion. At the start of the nineteenth century it was a simple sweet-smelling bunch of flowers of no set size, rejoicing in the apt name of 'nosegay'. From there it progressed to become a 'bouquet'; neat, solid and round-topped. The ones sold by Covent Garden florists were so solid that they were criticised for resembling cauliflowers. Mid-century there was a fashion for arranging flowers both for the hand and for vases, so that they all faced one way. These flat 'one-faced' constructions were easy for ladies to handle when travelling in their carriages as they could rest them on their knees, and indoors they could be laid down without fear of crushing. One-faced bouquets had a firm base, usually of Box or Fir, and a large solid flower (a white Dahlia was thought to look particularly fine) or a bunch

Waiting to be presented

(perhaps Roses) in the centre. Surrounding flowers might be Lilies, Passion Flowers, Azaleas or Geraniums. The latter two, because of their tendency to lose petals, benefited from a drop or two of isinglass. The flowers were mounted on stems of Willow or Green Hazel which was supple enough to be pushed through to the back of the bouquet and wired down. The vogue for one-faced bouquets was not enduring, many ladies preferring the conventional form.

At the end of the nineteenth century 'shower' bouquets became the rage. In these all the flowers faced more or less one way, rather as in one-faced bouquets, but were arranged in a long drooping cascade. This was more difficult to put together than earlier kinds. To make the job easier amateurs were advised to use long spikes of Orchid blossom.

The size of bouquets was tailored to fit the event. The largest, because it was usually carried only by a young lady being presented at Court, was known as a 'presentation' bouquet. Presentation involved the lady sweeping up with a trailing train through the Picture Gallery at Buckingham Palace and being announced on the threshold of the Throne Room by the Lord Chamberlain. There was, however, another avenue of presentation equally grand: afternoon 'drawing rooms'. A lady wishing to present another lady (perhaps an aunt her niece) would

apply through the Lord Chamberlain's office to attend a drawing room and write down on a card: 'Miss Woode, by her aunt, Mrs Woode'. This would be read out to the Queen by the Lord Chamberlain when the girl entered the room. It wouldn't have been necessary for her aunt to have attended but she probably did, for in describing the occupants of carriages in the Mall *en route* to a drawing room, the *Illustrated London News* of 25 March 1870 reports: 'These ladies, immersed in waves of satin, lace, and tulle, with feathers, flowers, and diamonds to adorn their heads, are manifestly on their way to perform the most serious duty of life.'

Not surprisingly, expensive flowers were favoured in presentation bouquets. As young ladies tended to keep these bouquets until they faded, gardeners were advised, when making them, to extend the lady's pleasure for as long as possible by using lots of damp moss and keeping the flower stems long. The lady herself could encourage the bouquet's longevity by keeping it under a glass dome; she would turn it upside down every morning and pour water through the stems before putting it back under the dome.

Wedding bouquets were not quite so large as presentation ones but bigger than ball bouquets. Even when 'shower' bouquets became fashionable they were not, because of their unwieldiness, taken to balls. Ladies preferred instead the old-fashioned round-topped posy.

The making-up of bouquets, in particular those for balls, was not a job to be undertaken lightly. The techniques involved had to be observed and learned for, as *The Gardener's Assistant* (1859) pointed out, 'As well might a cook pretend to serve an omelette or to boil rice, who has never seen it done by an experienced person.' The first step was to 'wire' the flowers. 'Stub' wire was used for artificial stems, a fine wire was employed to support flower heads and an even finer one to bind moss on to natural stems. The mossed flowers could then be put into tall jars of water in a cool dark cupboard to give time for the moss to soak up as much water as it would hold. A quantity of moss was also put into a container in water and left. When the time came to make up the bouquet, a bunch of moss of the thickness of a wrist was taken from the container, the central flower was put into the middle of it and a long piece of thread bound round the moss. The process was repeated with each flower, the amount of moss bound being regulated by the size of the flower. This wadding of moss helped to distance one flower from another and prevented the bouquet from looking 'crowded'. An outer edge of delicate fern fronds might be added and, if wanted, a flat perforated-paper fringe. The paper could in turn be covered with lace and neatly tied with satin ribbons an inch (2.5 cm) wide. The ribbons used on

Decorative paper fringes for bouquets

a ball bouquet should, according to *Domestic Floriculture*, be white 'with a little blue or pink worked in the bow'.

Ladies who wanted to make up their own bouquets were advised to use wire cornet-shaped frames which would support the flowers and also hold them slightly apart. This obviated the need to 'stub' every flower (fit it with a wire stalk which could be bent to keep one flower away from another). For those ambitious enough to make their own frames, a correspondent to the *Journal of Horticulture and Cottage Gardener* in July 1861 recommended, because it was easy to bend, silver wire, and for those worried about cost, came up with the helpful suggestion that it was less expensive if bought in French shops where rosaries were made.

Blue flowers were avoided in ball bouquets because they didn't look good under artificial light. If, as was often the case, the flowers had to match the dress and the dress were blue, ladies were advised to have flowers of a lighter rather than a darker shade of blue. For other dress colours, if the shade couldn't be exactly matched in flowers, it was better to have a similar lighter than a similar darker shade of flower. When there was no limit on colour, scarlet and white flowers were often favoured. An example of such a bouquet recommended in 1861 is: a white Rose or Geranium (in the centre) surrounded by white Deutzia or Cape Heath, single scarlet Anemones and dwarf 'Van Thol' single Tulips. There was a warning attached to this combination. The Tulips and Anemones would close in the dark or during a coldish drive but, happily, would open again in light and warmth. By candlelight their colours were said to look 'most beautiful'.

Similar well-meaning advice on the composition of bouquets is plentifully sprinkled through Victorian gardening journals. Below is a selection of advised 'dos' and 'don'ts':

DO

- Put Myrtle near the edge because even the slightest pressure from a touch brings out its fragrance.

- Include Sweetbriar and Lemon Scented Verbena (*Lippia citriodora*) for their scent but put them *under* the frame where they cannot be seen, because they look untidy.

- Sometimes edge with variegated foliage because it looks attractive.

- Make up a bouquet of very dark flowers to go against a black costume. Light-coloured flowers look poor against black but dark flowers are distinctly seen. Add a few bright leaves to catch the light.

🌹 Favour bouquets of Tea Roses arranged with their own foliage – these look beautiful, don't require wires and keep fresh for days.

🌹 Try pink or soft rose and pale-blue Forget-me-Nots: especially effective if margined with silvery Rhodanthes and elegantly fringed with Fern.

DON'T

🌿 Use Fuchsias, for they drop when carried and get crushed if drooping.

🌿 Use Heliotrope because it turns black so soon.

🌿 Use Ivy-leaved Geraniums because they give out a sickly smell when torn.

Domestic Floriculture notes that the fair possessor of a bouquet often enclosed its base in 'a jewelled horn of plenty, the gems of which scintillate and sparkle like all the dews of Golconda combined'. This showy description fitted perfectly several Victorian bouquet holders we were lucky enough to borrow for the television series. Harry, who was standing by to make bouquets for the half-dozen or so actresses who were to carry them, was heartily relieved when he saw these bouquet holders. He had been scratching his head over where he was going to find sufficient flowers of the right colour to match each actress' dress, each bouquet to be the size of a tea plate. However, when the bouquet holders arrived it was obvious that he could contract operations to saucer-size and possibly even smaller, the holders were so beautifully diminutive. Some were made totally of delicate gold or silver filigree, others had mother-of-pearl handles. Some handles were curved, some were straight but tapering, and others had three small legs tucked against them – at the touch of a button these splayed out and allowed the holder to be stood upright on a table. All had, attached to the base, a chain ending in a ring which a lady could slip on to her thumb or finger to hold the bouquet while she danced. Most had a pin on a chain which, when pushed through the cup, secured the flower stems inside. A few had 'jaws' which clamped together to hold the stems firm.

However, the most interesting holders were two which had additional 'social' uses. One bore a set of small ivory cards which fanned out from a point just below the cup of the holder. Some of the cards displayed evidence of their intended use, the pencilled-in names of gentlemen who once, on a night long ago, looked forward to the dance they had been promised. The other bouquet holder had a mirror, the size of a medium cameo, on each side. When the mirror was held up it reflected a 'receded' image and showed the whole room to the side of or behind the holder. What better discreet accessory could a chaperone have? Even with her back turned she could still keep her charge under scrutiny.

Should the young lady under surveillance be conversant with The Language of Flowers ('a genial exercise of poetic sentiment and memory'), though, she might have been a match for the receding mirror. For with a little forethought she might have laced her bouquet with a few extra useful flowers. An Ivy-leaved Geranium could come in very handy for some discreet flirting, provided that she could bear the smell (see the list of bouquet 'don'ts' on page 172). This, surreptitiously handed to a gentleman, meant: 'I engage you for the next dance.' What gentleman could refuse? A Phlox ('our souls are united') could be useful for the odd passionate pleasantry. Chinese Chrysanthemums ('cheerfulness under adversity') might also have been appropriate under such circumstances.

She in turn could receive from a gentleman a Scarlet Ipomoea ('I attach myself to you') – rather alarming if not welcome and she hadn't a striped Pink ('refusal') with which to reply. He might have to wait until next day when she could send him an Iceplant ('rejected addresses') or, wishing to be more emphatic, a Cactus ('horror'). This interesting floral language could go to deeper subtleties. If, when a flower was given, it was inclined to the left, it meant 'I'; inclined to the right, it meant 'thou'. Answering a question by giving a flower presented with the left hand meant 'no'; with the right, 'yes'. (More details on the 'moral property' of flowers are given inside the front cover.)

Welcome advances might lead, naturally, to a wedding, an event which not only had its share of floral symbolism but also involved a considerable amount of flowers. *Manners and Tone of Good Society or Solecisms to be Avoided* (*circa* 1875) states that under no circumstances should wedding guests carry bouquets, 'this being the privilege of the bride and bridesmaids only'; further, that the provision of the bride's and bridesmaids' bouquets is the bridegroom's responsibility and he must make sure that they are sent to the ladies individually on the morning of the wedding. This being so, it was presumably Albert Edward, Prince of Wales, who instructed Chelsea nurseryman James Veitch to make up the bouquet for his bride, Alexandra Caroline Maria of Denmark, and which Mr Veitch personally delivered to Windsor Castle on Sunday, 8 March 1863 (two days before the wedding, but perhaps they had to practise). Albert's mother, Queen Victoria, did however have a hand in this, for by her request the bouquet contained sprigs of Myrtle.

The Myrtle had been sent from Osborne House on the Isle of Wight. It had been gathered there from a tree which had been grown from a

Above right: Dress garlands of Bourbon Roses and a corsage spray containing a pale pink Rose. Harry's choice for the actress in a scene from the television series

Above: Stephanotis, Lilies and white Roses for the lady. A Gardenia buttonhole for the gentleman

Left: 'At the Ball' by Auguste François Gorguet (1862–1927)

sprig of Myrtle taken from the Princess Royal's wedding bouquet some six years earlier. As Queen Victoria made it known that she wished similar trees to be raised at Osborne from the Myrtle sprays of the marriage bouquets of each member of the royal family, a sprig must have been returned to Osborne. When Lady Diana Spencer (the present Princess of Wales) married Prince Charles, Myrtle was sent from Osborne to be included in her bouquet. Queen Victoria bought Osborne House in 1845, five years after her own wedding, so presumably no Myrtle tree was raised there from her own bouquet. However, at Fulham Palace, which was the home of the Bishop of London from Saxon times up until 1973, there are four Myrtle bushes. They are growing against the east front of the palace and, although clipped down to a moderate height, their trunks show evidence of age. It is said that *these* Myrtle bushes are the results of cuttings taken from Queen Victoria's wedding bouquet.

According to the Victorians' Language of Flowers, Myrtle means either 'love' or 'love in absence'. Perhaps it gained this symbolism from the knowledge that the Romans decorated Venus' altar with Myrtle. The practice of including it in wedding decorations was not confined to Britain. An 1870s' account relates how popular it was with German brides. A girl grew her own plant for making into a wreath for her head on her wedding day and if she died unmarried the Myrtle furnished her *Totenkranz* (wreath around her head when she lay in her coffin).

There is a final salutary tale about this Victorian symbol of love. At a court in Edinburgh in 1874 a lady claimed 'a sentimental grievance' against her clergyman tenant. He had ruthlessly pruned a Myrtle bush in her conservatory because it was overshading his own plants. The bush had been struck from a cutting from her wedding bouquet and the conservatory had been specially built to protect it as it grew. Her grievance was upheld and the clergyman was fined £10. The mutilated Myrtle lived to put forth fresh branches.

Flowering branch of Myrtle

On the subject of striking cuttings to commemorate weddings, if the groom had worn a Gardenia in his buttonhole there would have been no problem for, according to *The Garden* (3 November 1873), there are few plants more easily propagated. Harry, when told about the custom for striking Myrtle, didn't give it the same success rating. He said that Myrtle cuttings have a habit of not always striking root and he wouldn't have been surprised if a number of the young ladies years ago who thought they'd got a Myrtle bush in the garden which had sprung from their wedding bouquet were in fact looking at a cutting the gardener had got from quite a different source!

Below: Four Myrtle bushes (centre) growing against the east front of Fulham Palace

Victorian wedding-bouquet flowers were usually white to signify purity and chastity, although a mixture of yellow and white would not have been frowned upon. If yellow and white were wanted, the *Coelogyne cristata* Orchid with its gold-and-white bloom was particularly appropriate, as were buds of pale yellow to apricot Tea Roses. A favourite flower for the centre of the bouquet was *Eucharis amazonica* (introduced from New Granada in 1854). It has a heavy scent and white waxy blooms and gardeners valued it for the length of time it would flower. John Sayers, gardener, of Rockville, County Dublin, wrote to the *Journal of Horticulture and Cottage Gardener* in April 1873 to say that the pots of *Eucharis amazonica* in his garden had flowered for 314 days out of 366 (1872 was a leap year). Harry recalls that it used to grow thickly under the show house staging at Chilton and flower its head off. The situation was ideal for it – warm because it was near the hot-water pipes and damp because the floor was washed frequently.

Other traditional bridal-bouquet flowers were white Roses, white Carnations, white Orchids and a few sprays of Orange blossom. If Orange blossom (symbolic meaning 'purity') never found its way into the bouquet, it would without doubt have found its way, perhaps with other small white flowers, on to the bride's head. This custom was not liked by all. In 1873 Jeaffreson wrote in his book *Brides and Bridals*:

> The large, colourless crown never brightens, usually lowers the effects of a bride's beauty. Not one lovely girl in a thousand can wear it without disadvantage to her good looks. Custom and romance have raised the chaplet of orange-blossom to unmerited respect. The white of the orange-flower is an impure white, and the symbolism of the plant is a reason why some other flower should be adopted by the English bride.

Jeaffreson favoured a return to the days when brides wore wreaths of brightly coloured flowers. Despite this criticism, brides continued to wear Orange blossom not only in their hair but also on their dresses in either bunches or garlands. Perhaps it was Princess Alexandra who really set the seal on the fashion for wearing Orange blossom on a wedding dress: hers, in 1863, had five wreaths of it. One wonders if Mr Veitch delivered this decoration at the same time as her wedding bouquet. If not and it was made by the gardener at Windsor, he is an unsung hero, for when Harry made one garland he was up with the dawn, binding Smilax around the base of the garland and wiring on small bunches of Orange blossom. The bunches obstinately wanted to turn their blossoms downwards so that only half of the underside of the petals could be seen and it took practice to get them to sit properly. It is a good job that he

Left: The bride's floral adornment. Dress garlands of Orange blossom, headdress of Orange blossom and Gardenia, corsage spray of white Roses and Stephanotis, bouquet of white Carnations, Lilies, Stephanotis, 'Boule de Neige' Rose, Myrtle and Honiton lace. The groom wears a Gardenia buttonhole backed by its own leaves

Right: The bridesmaid carries a basket of old-fashioned pink and mauve Sweet Peas, pink Roses, Gladiolus 'The Bride', and pink sprays of Larkspur. She has Sweet Peas in her bonnet

Below: Orange blossom – symbolic meaning 'purity'

didn't have to do *five* such garlands and that the recipient was a bemused actress in Chilton church and not a royal princess at St George's Chapel, Windsor, for, what with all the other 'wedding' flowers he had to prepare that morning, things might have got a bit frenetic.

Tiny Victorian bridesmaids sometimes carried their flowers in what were called long-handled French baskets. Older girls had bouquets. A bridesmaid's flowers differed only from the bride's in that she was allowed some colour, generally to match her dress, but for the most part the flowers she wore or carried would have been white.

Coachmen arriving with the family and guests wore large buttonhole bouquets but gentlemen guests wore no buttonholes, leaving the lapel free for a wedding favour. Favours were distributed by the bridesmaids when the bride and groom had moved into the vestry to sign the register. For gentlemen they took the form of silver oak leaves and an acorn; for ladies a sprig of Orange blossom with silver leaves and white satin bows. Both ladies and gentlemen fixed their favour to the left side of their coat or bodice. If the bride were a widow she wasn't allowed favours, which is just as well as distribution could have been difficult because she wasn't allowed bridesmaids. It was also incorrect for widows to wear Orange blossom.

At society weddings in country villages children scattered flowers in the path of the bride as she walked from the church to her carriage. On arrival back at the bride's parental home, guests assembling in the drawing room prior to being ushered in to the wedding breakfast could admire wedding gifts displayed on tables. Couples lucky enough to receive many valuable presents often gave an afternoon tea the day before the wedding specifically for viewing purposes. *Manners and Tone of Good Society* considered it 'a pretty fashion to surround the presents with flowers, notably Roses, and this is often done by persons of artistic tastes'.

A well-bred Victorian bride did not, it seems, toss her bouquet into the air to be caught by an eager bridesmaid. Neither was it correct for her to put the flowers under a glass dome as a drawing-room ornament (to do the same with the wedding-cake ornaments was considered even more vulgar). Presumably the bouquet faded gently in a vase – apart, that is, from the sprigs of Myrtle which the gardener was called upon to immortalise, or appear to do so.

CHAPTER FOURTEEN
Alpines, Rocks and Ferns

Alpine flowers and false mountains – Rock gardens and painting them –
Pulham & Son, 'naturalistic' rock makers – 'The Acacias' Fernery – A Fern
museum – Fern hunters – Potting a Tree Fern mid-trunk – A Fern re-found.

Luncheon guests sitting and drinking coffee outside a house called The Friars were horrified when they saw two men, in a rowing boat on the lake, stand up, have a heated argument and both fall overboard. Sir Frank Crisp, the owner of The Friars, calmly remarked: 'I am very sorry to lose those men. Won't you have some more coffee?'

Only later did the guests find out that the lake was a trick. It had a partition half-way across. The men had fallen out of the boat over this and into 18 inches of water where they'd crawled out of sight.

This story was told in 1936 by Lord Aberconway at a conference on rock gardens. Frank Crisp had died in 1919 but was honourably mentioned at the conference for, in addition to trick lakes, he had a most extraordinary rock garden. Work on it began in the 1890s and the finished product was topped by a 30-foot (9-m) scale model of the Matterhorn, an unusual sight in Henley on Thames. The masses of vivid

Below: Sir Frank Crisp

Below right: The 'Matterhorn'
at Henley

alpine flowers which grew among the rocks below had been an equally unusual sight, for alpine flowers had not, it seems, until that point had happy associations with rock gardens.

This is odd because they appear to have got off to a good start. Mrs Loudon, in her *Practical Instructions in Gardening for Ladies* (1841), writes of a Lady Broughton successfully growing nothing but alpines on her rock work. Lady Broughton (like Sir Frank) had a rock garden on a large scale. It was a replica of the mountains of Savoy, with the valley of Chamonix. The rocks were made sufficiently large to give a person walking through the feeling that they were in the Alps. Lady Broughton designed it entirely herself and during the 1820s it had taken six to eight years to complete. Around her alpine plants, which had come from cool elevations, she ingeniously placed white stones to reflect the heat, and around those which needed warmth, black stones to absorb it.

Other gardeners at this time were putting their alpine plants into garden frames in the winter and covering them over with mats. This was to imitate their natural winter treatment on native mountains where they were covered with snow for months and 'excluded from atmospheric changes'. Indeed, alpines had a reputation for needing special treatment and being difficult. This was reinforced when they expired in rockwork of a less grand nature than Lady Broughton's mountains. During the middle part of the century these other rock gardens began to appear beside suburban houses. Leaving aside their apparent unsuitability for alpines, they made, it is said, a useful windbreak for the front door. Their construction invariably involved obtaining a pile of burrs (bricks which had fused together in baking at the brickyard), a quantity of broken fire clay from the gasworks and some chalk. All were broken down into irregular chunks and cemented together. To make the structure more 'rock-like' it was given a thin coat of cement. This could either be painted with 'Brunswick green', so that the whole looked mossy, or have lines of imitation rock strata painted on to it. Lime, water, oil and ochres of various shades were a useful mixture for the latter operation. As a final touch the whole could be decorated with plaster-casts (generally broken, hence their relegation to the garden), oyster shells and the remains of bottles and teacups. In 1870 *The Household Mechanic* advised against the last additions, considering them to be 'vulgarities'. Also in 1870 William Robinson, in a book called *Alpine Flowers*, recommended abandoning this sort of rockery altogether. He wrote:

Nearly the whole of the misfortunes which these little plants have met with in our gardens are to be attributed to a false conception of what a rockwork ought to be, and of what the true alpine plant requires. These plants live on high mountains; therefore it is thought they will do best in our gardens if elevated on such tiny heaps of stones and brick rubbish as we pile together and dignify by the name of 'rockwork'.

He goes on to point out that the trouble lay in alpine plants being put into a handful of soil which had been stuffed into a chink between the stones. The soil soon dried out and the plants died. However, he claimed that alpines in the wild flourished because they put their roots deep down into ravines filled with crumbled grit and soil.

In 1883, in his book *The English Flower Garden*, Robinson was criticising another form of rockwork for a similar reason: the large masses of artificial rocks commissioned by the wealthy owners of country estates. He believed that the 'pockets' made in them for soil were so small that they starved the plants. This may have been a rather sweeping observation, for the *Gardeners' Magazine* of 15 September 1888 reports well of a huge mass of artificial rocks at Madresfield Court in Worcestershire:

> The imitation is so perfect that we have to assure ourselves of its artificiality, the great blocks being so admirably modelled, and the dislocations adapted for the accommodation of plants, while having the complexion of perfect naturalness. The planting is sufficient to give richness and variety without overloading it, for a rockery should display its rocks, as well as its Ivies and Brambles and Junipers and Ferns, which are here delightfully represented, with many lovely alpines to make a botanists' paradise of the scene.

The Madresfield rocks had been designed and built by the firm of James Pulham & Son of Broxbourne in Hertfordshire. The firm prided itself that its rockwork bore no resemblance to the 'Cockney tea-garden style' of clinker and glass but was done in a 'proper naturalistic style'. On request, Mr Pulham or his son would travel to the estate of a prospective client to assess what style of rocks would suit. The client paid hotel and travelling expenses. If, after a plan was drawn up, it was accepted, the firm would send men and hire out tackle to haul to the site natural rock from the surrounding neighbourhood. If insufficient rock was found, or if, as sometimes happened, there was no natural rock, Mr Pulham's men artificially formed 'rocks' on the spot. They started with a core of rough bricks, covered them with cement and worked the cement so that it imitated the colour, form and texture of real rock. Their skills could turn out red, yellowish, grey or brown sandstone, limestone and tufa. The

rocks were joined by the cement, the joins being indistinguishable from pieces of stone.

The Madresfield 'rocks'

The cement they used was called Pulhamite (the name later became attached to stone-coloured terracotta ornaments the firm manufactured) and owed its origin to the father of James Pulham Senior, also called James. He had worked as a plasterer with a Norfolk builder called William Lockwood. In 1822 the two men had invented Portland cement, which was based on limestone and whose stone colour made it far more suitable for plaster work than Roman cement. Pulhamite is believed to have been an improvement on the original Portland cement. Its manufacture and application were important because the rocks had to withstand frost and water. Pulham's men were practised in its use, for, as theirs was a specialised skill, most had started with the firm as boy apprentices. At Madresfield they did their job well and the mini-Grand Canyon still stands, looking for all the world like real rocks. However, there is one rather touching clue that they are not what they seem. It is

An 1886 advertisement

CHRYSANTHEMUMS.—ADVERTISEMENTS.

Gentlemen contemplating Improvements in their Grounds, either in the Picturesque or Formal Styles,

SHOULD CONSULT

PULHAM & SON

AS TO THE INTRODUCTION OF THEIR

NATURALISTIC ROCK FORMATION

SO WELL ADAPTED FOR MARGINS TO

Lakes, Streams, and construction of Waterfalls,

Rock Gardens in Picturesque Scenery,

INSIDE OR OUTSIDE FERNERIES & PLANTARIA.

ALSO IN DESIGN AND EXECUTION OF

Balustrade, Terraces, Fountains, Vases, Jardiniere, Italian & Dutch Gardens, Sun-dials, &c.,

IN TERRA COTTA AND CONCRETE STONE.

THE PULHAMITE PERMANENT GRAVEL,

So well adapted for Walks, Conservatory, Fernery, Planthouse, Stable, Tennis Floors, &c.

CONSERVATORIES & WINTER GARDENS

Fitted up in Formal or Naturalistic Styles.

Photographs sent for Inspection of their various Works, on application, for 12 Stamps.

PULHAM & SON,

THE WORKS, BROXBOURNE.

Patronised by all the principal Landscapists and Architects since 1850; also H.R.H. the Prince of Wales, &c.

on a rock discreetly in a crevice and was recently uncovered by the present head gardener. While the cement on it was still wet, one of Pulham's men had scratched:

THIS WORK
By M. J. PULHAM
BROXBOURNE
A.D. 1878.79
WORKMEN
R. PEGRAM, BO2
J. 2TRACEY, J. JON2ON
FINI JULY 18.

The firm of Pulham was employed by Sir Frank Crisp of The Friars. Among other work they made the banks to the lake, and perhaps they also built its trick partition. (It was another company, Backhouse of York, famous for its alpines, which constructed the alpine landscape.) In 1895 Pulham & Son were granted a Royal Warrant of Appointment to HRH the Prince of Wales. It came about through having done work at Sandringham, although a swan might have also had something to do with the honour. Mr Arthur Pulham, now in his eighties and the last to carry the family name, told me that when his grandfather James went to supervise the work at Sandringham he rescued the Prince of Wales (later Edward VII) who was being attacked by a swan, and the men became friends.

Mr Arthur Pulham also kindly let me see a book which, although undated, appears to have been printed in the 1870s. It is by James Pulham and, being the author's rushed copy, unfortunately has blank spaces instead of pictures. Nevertheless the text is informative. It describes the making of a 'Naturalistic Pulhamite Fernery, Conservatory or Winter Garden' that involved constructing rocks and slopes which, despite being made inside walls already built, could look undulating and natural. A water cistern behind the rocks would supply water both for effect and for watering the ferns which would be planted to appear as though growing out of the rocks.

At Reading there is a Victorian house called The Acacias where the door to what may once have been the drawing room opens directly into a glasshouse. Anyone stepping out walks immediately between rocky slopes set with 'pockets' for plants. There are small water taps camouflaged by rockwork. It is thought that this is a Pulham Fernery, which

Right: The Acacias' Fernery

may well be true, for in his book James Pulham wrote a twenty-six-verse poem to such Ferneries and verse 22 seems to sum up The Acacias' sort nicely:

Aged votaries of nature can enjoy at home,
Small picturesque scenes in a ferny dell to roam,
View foliage, rock, and water, have changes of air,
And explore the whole round in a Bath chair.

Presumably after this they retired to the house and continued their sedentary appreciation by taking refreshment from a glass engraved with Fern fronds and eating from a dish painted with Fern varieties, using a spoon with a Fern-embossed back and sitting in a chair inlaid with mother-of-pearl Fern images. It *could* have happened, for manufacturers of household goods were quick to capitalise on 'Pteridomania' (alias the Fern Craze) which infected many Victorians from the 1850s until the end of the century.

There is a very fine collection of Fern-decorated objects in the Museum of North Devon in Barnstaple: Devon is a Ferny county. The collection is the inspiration of Peter Boyd, the museum's curator, who wanted to link the natural history of the area with its social history. Leaving aside the fascination of Fern-decorated Wedgwood cheese dishes, the museum also has books of pressed Ferns. Looking at the delicate shapes of the dried Ferns and the sometimes startling pages of gold and silver fronds which gain their natural colour from a coating of either yellow or white farinose powder, it is easy to see their fascination.

Victorian compilers of herbariums were advised to sew their specimens to the page rather than glue them, because insects attracted to the glue chewed through the specimens. Such was not the case with Ferns, which could safely be glued as herbarium-infesting insects didn't like these particular plants. This interesting Fern fact comes from a book written by George William Francis called *An Analysis of the British Ferns and their Allies*. First published in 1837, it no doubt helped to launch the Fern Craze. Francis states in the introduction that he wrote it because the only other book ever published on Ferns had long been out of print. He admits that the illustrations are his own first 'untutored attempt at etching' but explains that he did them himself because it saved expense which perhaps would not be recouped if the book did not sell. He was unnecessarily pessimistic, for by 1855 it was in its fifth edition. Part of its fascination to Victorian readers must have been in the fact that it gives details of the habitat of each Fern, often in surprising detail. For example, one particular Fern was to be found in a field behind Heawood Hall, Alderley, Cheshire; another on the tower of Old Alresford Church,

Buttonhole holder with Fern motif. The silver Fern leaf was clipped on the front of the buttonhole and the tube was hidden by the lapel

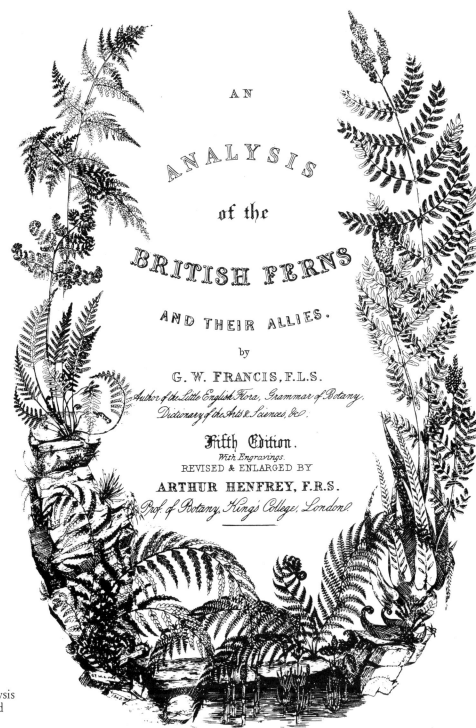

AN

ANALYSIS

of the

BRITISH FERNS

AND THEIR ALLIES,

by

G. W. FRANCIS, F.L.S.

Author of the Little English Flora, Grammar of Botany,
Dictionary of the Arts & Sciences, &c.

Fifth Edition.

With Engravings.

REVISED & ENLARGED BY

ARTHUR HENFREY, F.R.S.

Prof. of Botany, King's College, London.

Title page from An Analysis
of the British Ferns and
their Allies

Hampshire; and the tallest and most beautiful of British Ferns, *Osmunda regalis*, was, among other places, to be found 'sparingly' on Esher Common 'by the entrance to the lane leading thence towards Epsom'. No doubt its presence became even more 'sparing'.

George Francis also recommended growing Ferns in one of Nathaniel Ward's cases, explaining the principle of how plants in these were kept moist by condensation trickling down the inside of the glass. In the ensuing years there can have been few drawing rooms without Ferns in various forms of Wardian cases. As late as 1897 *Ferns and Fern Culture*, by J. Birkenhead, has several illustrations of Ferns growing in them.

The Fern Craze was fuelled by various factors. Improvements in transport systems encouraged tourism. A correspondent to the *Cottage Gardener and Country Gentleman* in 1858 wrote to report of his tour in Wales, during which he 'fell in with' some specimens of case Ferns: 'We brought home more than 100 young plants, and at this time many of them are flourishing famously in semi-Wardian cases.' An organised Fern hunt (permission was obtained for these after the pheasant-shooting season) provided a day's leisure, interesting lessons in nature and, at the end of the day, enough 'finds' to furnish a hardy Fernery. Open commons had an added piquancy. Cassell's *Popular Gardening* (*circa* 1880) remarks of them: 'To scamper over these basket and trowel in hand, no man daring to make the Fern-hunter afraid, is a high and satisfying pleasure.'

The cool greenness of a garden Fernery provided refuge for eyes dazzled by the brilliant colours of bedding plants and comfort for bodies made uncomfortably warm by garden hothouses.

Above: Fern stand and glass

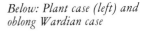

Below: Plant case (left) and oblong Wardian case

Ferns were also accommodating plants. Conservatories attached to town houses were often built in nooks and corners and were too dark to grow flowers well but Ferns thrived in them.

Ferns had one other important attraction. For no apparent reason one specimen could present a different appearance from its fellows of the same species. Some writers referred to this as the workings of an 'unknown natural force'. These oddities became greatly sought after. Sometimes they could be found in the wild; often they were raised from spores. They were seen by collectors as varieties in their own right. Edward Joseph Lowe, a great Fern enthusiast, wrote that the Fern culti-

Organised Fern hunts provided a day's leisure and 'finds' for a hardy Fernery

vator must include them among his choicest gems. Mr Lowe practised what he preached, for a journalist from *The Garden* visiting him in 1874 saw 15,000 different varieties of English Ferns, nearly all raised from spores, many of them being different varieties only in the connoisseur's eyes. There were:

> Ferns lovely, Ferns ugly, Ferns like fairy dreams, and Ferns like grim nightmares; Ferns tall, crested, broad, narrow, long, short, curled, straight, twisted like mosses, or split up into fronds as delicate as the Maiden-hair, and as unlike their normal form as anything can be. There are few horticultural sensations so great as the variety of Mr Lowe's Ferns.

In tandem with the interest in hardy British Ferns was an enthusiasm for kinds which required the protection of glass. These had at first a reputation for being difficult but it was discovered that many fared better when heat was modified. Imported living plants and, it is claimed, ones grown from spores taken from herbaria helped to swell their numbers. Tree Ferns were especially loved for their tropical appearance but, owing to their size, they needed a large Fernery or lofty conservatory. Nicholson's *Dictionary of Gardening* (1884) advised gardeners with limited space to restrict the root of a Tree Fern by keeping it in a large tub. This also enabled the Fern to be moved around when it began to overshadow other plants.

It was all sound advice, which Harry followed, and the Tree Fern at Chilton had its pot moved around until it finally rested at a point below the steps in the show house. As the year progressed it became apparent that this plant, happy with its situation, had put on an extra spurt of growth. It also became apparent that if its act of elevation continued, the Fern would start pushing into the roof glass. Harry decided that action had to be taken. He asked David to knock the bottom out of a large terracotta pot and then cut the pot in half vertically. It wasn't the easiest task that David had been given, particularly the halving; but, by dint of sawing and chipping, one side was eventually severed from the other.

Harry meanwhile took some loose fronds off the Fern so that he could get easily to its trunk. When David reappeared with the halved pot, Harry showed him thin black roots which emerged all the way up the trunk. What they would attempt to do, Harry explained, was to encourage the plant to develop those aerial roots. The technique involved in doing this has had a number of names: it used to be called 'Chinese layering' or 'marcottage' but today it is known as air layering. Giving David one end of a two-handled saw, Harry asked him to place the blade against the Fern trunk about mid-way down. Then very carefully they sawed until the trunk was cut half-way through. Taking out the saw, Harry placed one half of the cut flower pot against the Fern trunk so that the cut in the trunk came into line with the pot. David pushed the other half of the pot against the other side of the trunk until the two halves met. The halves were then lashed together with strong twine. The Fern presented a singular appearance: it had a flower pot at its base on the floor but appeared also to be growing out of another pot half-way up its trunk. It was exactly what Harry wanted. He filled the suspended pot with compost and then got David to help him build a scaffold of stakes tied with twine around the Fern trunk to stop it toppling. As he watered the compost Harry explained to David that when sufficient roots had grown into the suspended pot all the trunk beneath it could be cut away and the pot be lowered to floor height. The plant would then be half its original height.

The Tree Fern would stay in the show house, for even in its new diminutive state it would still be too big to join the collection of greenhouse Ferns Harry had built up. These were in a small span-roofed house parallel to the stovehouse. Like the Victorians, Harry valued a Fernery for its cool greenness, but he also appreciated it as a reservoir of camouflage. There was, he said, nothing better than a few pots of Ferns to hide defects, particularly when you were faced with the task of keeping the show house in flower and decorating the mansion the whole year through. A pot or two of Ferns was invaluable for concealing the base of a plant which had a good flower but went up on an unsightly leg, or for disguising a plant whose leaves were past their best. Maidenhair was particularly useful for the purpose, although Harry's predecessors would have had to use it with care because it didn't stand up well to the fumes given off by gas light. Despite this, it had a hundred years ago attracted the epithet 'Everybody's Fern', for it mixed well with cut flowers and in a pot was of accommodating medium growth. Harry's Fern house also had pots of *Asplenium bulbiferum* which earned its Victorian name of Parlour Fern because it did stand up to gas fumes.

A basket suspended from the roof held a Davallia. Its creeping stems, which tumbled over the side and beneath the basket, were covered in a pale fur. It must have been *Davallia tyermanni* for this has long had the common name Silver Squirrel's-foot. Stately *Osmunda regalis*, the Royal Fern, was hardy enough to feel at home in the cool Fern house but *Lygodium japonicum*, the climbing Japanese Fern, was transferred into more heat to encourage it to live up to its name. It joined *Polypodium aureum*, a handsome tropical Fern which had been introduced into Britain as long ago as 1742. Also coming along nicely in the stovehouse were pots of *Platycerium alcicorne*, more commonly known as

Asplenium fontanum, a favourite in hardy Ferneries

Stag's-horn Fern because it looks exactly like a stag's antlers. When his Stag's-horn grew large enough Harry planned to fix these extraordinary-looking plants on to blocks of cork and hang them up. Victorian Fern manuals noted that they were 'grand for suspending over a doorway'!

The Stag's-horns had been given to Harry by 'Matt' Busby of the British Pteridological Society. The society was feeling particularly Victorian as it was about to celebrate its centenary. It had been started by a group of Fern lovers who had met at the home of one of their number in Kendal, Cumbria, in 1891. They began what they called the Northern British Pteridological Society but which over the years has evolved into its present form. Matt, who is honorary general secretary, is proud to have made the last entry in the original minute book of the society. A new book was started, for the society flourishes.

Matt seemed a good person to ask where we could get a favourite Victorian Fern called *Nephrodium fragrans*. It had been introduced from North America in 1820 and its attraction lay in its scent, which *The Garden* of 3 August 1878 described as 'much resembling, but superior to that of Violet blossom'. However, it seems that unfortunately this Fern is not to be found anywhere. If it had been easily obtainable, it is certain that the society would know, for its members have a nose for such things. Recently, a member tracked down a Lady Fern called *Athyrium filix femina* 'Victoriae'. This Fern had been originally discovered in 1861 growing wild by a stone dyke near Drymen in Stirlingshire. It was so beautiful that it was honoured with the Queen's name. Owing to the formation of its delicate lattice work frondage the Fern was considered unique. It is still considered to be so, for no Fern found since is similar in design. Disappointingly, over the years, none of its progeny has matched the original Victoriae for size and beauty. Indeed, it looked as though the reputation of that first plant would remain legend. Then in 1989 Pteridologist Nick Schroder discovered an unusually fine example of Victoriae in a garden near Dryden. Its owner explained that the fern had once belonged to his father and it could be traced back to having started life as a piece from the original Victoriae found in 1861! For safety, a bit of the rediscovered Victoriae has been lodged with the National Fern Collection, Saville Gardens, Windsor.

Previous pages: Harry and David 'shortening the Tree Fern (left) and the Fern house at Chilton

Platycerium alcicorne *(the Stag's-horn Fern)*

CHAPTER FIFTEEN

Decorating the Mansion

There is a leather label hung on a nail in the gloomy but useful annexe room which leads to Harry's office. The room is useful because its benches act as assembly points for garden produce destined for dispatch. Each day in the rough roadway outside a car or two pulls up and its owner climbs out to collect his or her order. Some drivers are shop keepers, others private individuals who have houses big enough to need mansion-size house plants but no longer have gardeners to supply them. The leather label remains untouched. It belongs to another era, to the days when the gardens' pony shook its harness by the doorway and huge wicker hampers creaked as their leather straps were tightened up a notch. *Then* the label would have been taken from its hook, turned to show, cut clearly into the leather, an address in Park Lane, London, and carefully attached to one of the hampers.

Along with its fellows the hamper would be placed into the waiting gardens' wagon and the pony would trot them to the local railway station. Here they would be set down in readiness to be put aboard the next London-bound train. Before returning, the drivers of the wagon would load empty hampers. Their arrival at the railway station had been directed by the leather labels reversed so that 'Park Lane' was turned inwards and they showed on their outer face the address of the gardens.

If the full hampers were put into the goods wagon of a nine o'clock train, by noon a footman at the London house could be opening them and taking out fresh vegetables for the cook, choice fruit for the butler's pantry and carefully packed cut flowers for room decoration.

This shuttle service, which allowed the mansion owners to enjoy fresh produce from their country estate even when they were staying at their London residence, was still in practice when Harry took up his job as head gardener. He carried it on, not using the leather labels but still using the old produce hampers.

On the flowers side it was, he remembers, always cut flowers which were dispatched, not pot plants. The only exception to this was pot plants which happened to be in flower at the time the owners were leaving the mansion. On request as to which of these were required, Harry packed them up and they were taken together with other luggage. In the normal course of events flowers were usually cut the evening before and stood in deep water in a cool spot. First thing in the morning they were packed into special hampers. These had wires sticking inwards from the four corners, supporting a wickerwork tray. In the main body of the basket Harry used to put what he calls substantial flowers: Chrysanthemums, Dahlias and Gladioli. The tray held delicate Sweet Peas, Freesias, Violets or Carnations. Harry recalls that before the Second World War many gardens had special cardboard boxes for dispatching flowers. The cardboard, which was very stiff, was known as 'leatherboard'. The boxes were in varying degrees of shallowness; most were 6 inches (15 cm) deep which meant that often it was possible to put in only a single layer of flowers. Gladiolus were cut and packed while still in bud.

Whatever their container, Harry says that it was important to pack the flowers tight without crushing them. The usual way of doing this was, starting with the longest-stemmed ones, to put some with the blooms at one end, and some the other, and work inwards from both ends with stems of decreasing length. Invariably you were left with a gap in the middle, but a 'bolster' (a wad of rolled paper) placed in the gap not only held the stalks firm but also, if large enough, stopped the lid crushing the flowers. A stick wedged widthways across the container also helped to hold the stems in place.

When the family was at their country residence, the demand for flowers took on a different aspect. In the early days Harry recalls four-legged garden handcarts being loaded with pot plants. Protective materials could be put round them to shield tender plants on the journey from the walled kitchen gardens to the mansion. Flowers were cut early in the morning while the dew was still on them. Dahlias and Roses and other flowers which held a lot of moisture were shaken. The method for this, Harry says, is to hold the bunch up to about shoulder level and bring it down with a swish. The follow through will take the bunch half of that height behind your back and that's usually sufficient to get rid of heavy surplus.

Decorating the mansion with flowers was a job the head gardener usually undertook. Harry's first experience of it started at the reverse end. In the days before he left school at Blackmoor he went with his Uncle Fred and the garden foreman to clear vases of flowers away after the owners and their guests had left the rooms. At that time he was more at home in the mansion kitchens collecting the cook's produce order and carrying baskets of fruits and vegetables back to her.

When Harry was a journeyman at Stansted Park he held the cut-flower box while the head gardener, Mr Tomalin, cut flowers and he also helped to carry flowers to the mansion. He didn't assist with the decoration inside; that was the province of Mr Tomalin, assisted by the inside foreman and the third journeyman (the man immediately below the foreman). Mr Tomalin, whom Harry held in awe, was more than proficient at the task. In days gone by, Harry remembers, some large gardens had a young man who was known as 'the decorator'. It was his job to do mansion floral decorations and in between times work around the glasshouses. Mr Tomalin had first joined the Bessborough family as a decorator and worked his way up.

When flowers first arrived from the garden they didn't go to the rooms where they would be displayed. Instead they went to a flower room. Harry has seen flower rooms which were adequate for their task – they contained the necessary wooden sink, water supply and benches on which to arrange vases – but which were grim. Some were deep in the basement or at the farthest end of the mansion, which meant that any flowers carefully arranged at the outset of their journey from the flower room had to be touched up before being finally put into place. Harry says that after the Second World War, when garden staff was not so plentiful, the lady of the house often took a greater interest in flower arranging and then flower rooms became much more accessible and brighter places as they were converted from rooms which had been used for other purposes. Times changed in other respects too. In pre-war days the head gardener (or decorator) used to be at his task in the mansion before seven o'clock in the morning and was expected to be out by half-past nine before the gentry were about. After the war the earliest he could get into the mansion was nine o'clock and sometimes he would still be helping the lady set flowers at noon.

An important item in the flower room was a pair of slippers. These were always provided for the head gardener. Harry recalls that no self-respecting gardener would ever go into any of the apartments without having first taken off his boots in the flower room and donned the slippers. Even today if he went into the house he would immediately take off his boots: it was something he was taught to do at an early age. Care for the surroundings also manifest itself in other ways. Lilies had to have the yellow anthers removed from their trumpets, not only to stop them fading once pollen dropped on to the stigma but also to prevent the pollen falling out and staining carpets or delicate fabric on furniture. Any beads of moisture on a watering can were carefully wiped off and if foli-

Overleaf: A young lady in her boudoir, 1865; Begonia 'Gloire de Lorraine' (top right); Cyclamen persicum

age fell from the butler's tray, the usual conveyance for filled vases, it
had to be quickly picked up. If, when the vases were placed, petals
or leaves fell on to a table which contained a lot of ornaments, Harry
says that you told the housemaids you were sorry and they would clear it
for you.

The relationship between gardeners and housemaid was not so cordial over Pileas. These are small plants with insignificant flowers but Fern-like foliage which was useful for disguising the containers of larger plants. They were also known as Artillery Plants because, when their tiny flowers are fully open the slightest touch makes the anthers burst releasing a charge of pollen. Some young journeymen assisting with flower decorating would surreptitiously flick the odd flower, much to the annoyance of the housemaids, for it was, Harry says, 'a miserable little thing to clear off the carpets'. This activity gave the plant a third name: Housemaid's Delight.

Gardeners were always taught that only the lightest and most elegant flower arrangements were placed in a lady's boudoir. Harry remembers that a special favourite was *Iris stylosa*. This Iris has azure-blue flowers on stems of about 6 inches (15 cm). It was referred to in 1874 as 'a novelty' and 'not long since appeared in catalogues'. Clumps of *Iris stylosa* planted in the shelter of a warm wall will come into bud in the snow of mid-winter. Harry used to cut one or two buds and put them into water in a warm glasshouse. In a short while they would open out and the scented flowers be ready for placing in a lady's room. Small vases of other sweet-smelling flowers were appropriate too, but each vase was restricted to one kind of flower. Bowls of Snowdrops, Lily-of-the-Valley, *Cyclamen persicum* and pots of *Begonia* 'Gloire de Lorraine' were also acceptable. The Begonia had small, rosy pink flowers which glowed under artificial light. Harry remembers that some gardeners years ago had whole houses of this Begonia, all of which had to be staked and tied. It was a difficult plant. Cuttings were not rooted until April and then they had to be looked after until November when they flowered. After they died down they still had to be kept in heat and watering was a problem because it took experience and intuition not to make them too wet. It is hardly surprising that in the horticultural world there used to be a saying that you judge a gardener by his grapes, onions and *Begonia* 'Gloire de Lorraine'! Today, it's an even more difficult task to grace a boudoir with *Begonia* 'Gloire de Lorraine', for though it's still sold by wholesale propagators in Denmark there appears to be no supplier in Britain.

It is not so much flowers but good 'lasting foliage' that Cassell's *Popular Gardening* (1880) recommends for bedrooms and dressing rooms: a thoughtful touch, as they emphasise that 'in an emergency it can be taken for personal decoration with other flowers, if necessary'. Earlier Victorian publications reflect scant regard for bedroom decorations, particularly from men. A correspondent to the *Cottage Gardener and Country Gentleman* in 1857 believed that bedrooms were for sleeping, not lingering in, and vacating them with all speed was wise for too much sleep made the body 'effeminate' and 'like Mrs What's-her-name's tea, so weak that it could not run up the spout'.

The halls and corridors of Victorian mansions were beset (despite copious drapery) with draughts. This meant that only the hardiest of Palms would flourish in them without flagging. Aspidistra, Eucalyptus and large vases of Chrysanthemums were sturdy enough to survive. Temporary groups of bold striking-looking flowers were also favoured: Delphiniums, Lilies, Gladioli, *Salvia splendens* and *Eucharis amazonica*. If flowers were scarce, displays could be supplemented with Pampas and other tall grasses. A useful suggestion by one manual to gardeners is to take *Celosia pyramidalis* into the hall when its root and stem are too faded for conservatory decoration. The fluffy coloured tops (often likened to ostrich feathers) would look well and the stems could be hidden if it was placed at the back of a group.

There could have been an exchange of currency with the conservatory for the Chimney Bell-flower (*Campanula pyramidalis*), when it had done its stint in a hall or corridor, could by dint of a bit of restoration work be given another lease of life. This tall Campanula – if cosseted with liquid farmyard manure it could grow up to 7 feet (2 m) – would re-flower if a gardener took the trouble to cut off all the dead blooms. Harry called this task 'a quiet job'; it took time because, when they were cut, the faded flowers exuded a sticky substance which stuck to the slender blades of garden scissors, but despite this many a lad found it preferable to going out into the garden to dig. Few private gardens nowadays bother to grow this plant. Another neglected tall pot plant is *Humea elegans*. *Hooper's Gardening Guide* (*circa* 1896) calls it elegant and describes it as having profuse, drooping, red panicles and leaves which exhale 'a strong aromatic odour'. Hostesses in days gone by had it placed in corridors outside the gentlemen's cloakroom.

Drawing-room mantelpieces, warmed by a fire below, were extravagant places for fresh blooms. Victorian ladies who valued economy saw to it that these shelves looked bright with small glass vases filled with dried flowers. Their papery petals could be made to smell sweet with a droplet of an appropriate essential oil, such as oil of Cloves on Pinks and oil of Roses on Roses. A bigger vase filled with everlasting flowers, dried grasses and seed pods could be made even more everlasting by covering with a glass dome to prevent fading. Domes were essential to keep off dust when an everlasting bouquet had been given a sparkle of alum crystals. This was done by dipping it into a solution of hot water and alum powder and then hanging it up to dry.

Dishes of flowers seemed to be favoured in the mid-nineteenth century. When Harry decorated a drawing room for the television series he

Right: Harry dead-heading a Chimney Bell-flower. A 'quiet job'

A mantelpiece garden

followed instructions given in an 1861 gardeners' journal for a drawing-room table dish. The base was a large crystal dish filled with water. The edges were to be fringed with Fern and, working inwards (the advised best method), a double row of pale pink full-blown Roses followed by Passion Flowers which should seem 'to float upon the water'. An optional extra was a tall glass tumbler placed in the centre of the dish and filled with a knot of drooping flowers and foliage (Fuchsias and trailing Ferns worked well in this), and at the base of the tumbler a wreath of the same pink Roses. The finished result did look lovely and one could see the attraction of looking down on to the blue Passion Flowers. There is, however, a problem with this design: Passion Flowers stay open for only one day and indeed can start to close up forever by later afternoon. They can also be spasmodic in their appearance in the garden, for sometimes a number appear, sometimes only one or two, so collecting sufficient can be difficult. There is a solution to both these problems: it is not explained in the 1861 design instructions but it does appear in Cassell's *Popular Gardening*. The secret of success lies in cutting the flowers early in the morning when they are fully out and putting them into darkness. They will keep open for up to five days in the dark, so extra ones can be cut and added each day until enough have been gathered. If the drawing-room dish were wanted especially for the evening, the Passion Flowers had to be brought out of the dark just before they were needed.

Other 'flowers of a day' required for evenings, such as Ipomoea (Morning Glory), also had to be kept dark during the day. Water Lilies could be made to keep open at night by passing a finger and thumb up each petal and reflexing it.

Dish designs which were flat – that is, not in a bowl but more on a plate scale – could run into problems if in the heat of the room the outer edges of foliage (flowers on an outer edge were considered too 'heavy') curled up. One Victorian lady wrote the following recipe for an unwilting edge: 'For many years we used a common soup-plate set on an embroidered stand, with a thick edge of moss-like wool, knitted, boiled, baked, let cool, and untwisted, and this looks less objectionable than might have been supposed.'

Fairly heavy-looking vases could be used for drawing-room flowers. Sand, damp enough to supply moisture but not so wet that it wouldn't hold the flowers in position, went in as foundation. To avoid it being seen from above it was covered with green moss. If the vase were glass, the whole of the inside had to be lined with moss before the sand went in. Sprigs of evergreen, such as Box-leaved Myrtle, Bay or Common Box, could be used as an alternative to the moss. Some thought this superior, for if a graceful green spray 'surfaced' it would not look out of place among the flowers. During the last quarter of Victoria's reign canons of taste appear to have specified that no two vases in the same room should be filled with the same flowers and that the colour of vases themselves had to be given consideration. Gaudy reds and blues were never to be used for delicately coloured flowers but instead bronze, black or dark green vases. For dark-coloured flowers a pale vase was necessary.

Arrangement of flowers in vases varied. In the early 1860s there is advice that a dense mass of flowers containing every colour of the rainbow could look well if tastefully arranged. Towards the end of the 1870s flowers are recommended to be grouped with their own kind in a vase or, if mixed, that the vase should be divided into sections and each section made to harmonise within itself and be blended with its fellow sections by lines of green and neutral tints. Baskets of flowers, particularly if they contained spring bulbs, were consistently popular.

Single plants in drawing rooms were chosen for beauty of foliage. Variegated Aspidistras, small Crotons, Caladiums and *Alocasia metallica* rated highly. Also apparent favourites were plants with scented foliage such as *Lippia citriodora* Verbena and Geraniums with scented leaves. If plants turned sickly, the fumes of gas could be conveniently blamed but some sources accuse servants who, by flinging windows open wide when they cleaned early in the morning, subjected plants to icy draughts. Tender forced plants were particularly susceptible to this treatment.

One plant which could withstand practically any treatment was Ivy. A writer in an 1875 edition of *The Garden* states: 'I do not know a single plant that will stand so much hard usage as Ivy.' Indeed, it was hard used. Wedge-shaped tin receptacles were planted up with Ivies and put on nails *behind* pictures and mirrors, the object being to make them trail gracefully over and around the frames. The *Villa Gardener* of August 1870 says of Ivy: 'In France and particularly about Paris, where the latest fashion reigns, it is made to do the duty of appearing as a living screen in a drawing room.' A useful engraving is shown to help those wishing to emulate the fashion.

Ivy also came into its own at grand events. On one occasion in 1874, 2 tons of it were used at the Mansion House in London to drape pictures, mirrors and walls. All types of evergreens were popular as temporary decoration for public function rooms. They were made into wreaths and festoons for walls and balconies. Suitable monograms were often pinned on to them.

The fashion for flowering plants and shrubs at balls began to make itself apparent in the 1840s. The *Quarterly Review* reported: 'No dread of "noxious exhalations" deters mammas from decorating their halls and stair cases with flowers of every hue and fragrance, nor their daughters from braving the headaches and pale cheeks which are *said* to arise from such innocent and beautiful causes.' This trend had progressed to such an extent that *Domestic Floriculture* (1874) recommended that the staircase be covered with crimson baize and be fringed on each side with Ferns, Isolepis, Palms and flowering plants. It commented on the prevailing fashion for corners of ballrooms to be decorated with groups of graceful Ferns, Palms, Cycads and Yuccas and suggested that, in addition to the usual wreathing of Ivy festoons, flat bouquets of flowers be fixed under gas brackets; all this plus choice flowers in distinct colours grouped beneath graceful Palms and beside statues.

Professional 'floral decorators' were called in to mastermind the decor of the grandest functions. Below is a description of what could be achieved:

Above: Ivy emanating from a wedge-shaped tin behind a mirror

> At a ball given by the Prince and Princess of Wales to the Czarevna of Russia in the large conservatory of the Royal Horticultural Society at South Kensington, ten tons of the finest ice were employed in building an illuminated rockery. This was draped with drooping Ferns and graceful trailers, while the base was fringed with slender-growing Ferns and small pots of Isolepis gracilis and Selaginella. The effect of the whole when surrounded by crimson baize and illuminated from within was strikingly effective and much admired.

Harry followed instructions in an 1861 manual to make this drawing-room table dish. It includes Passion Flower heads floating on water surrounded by full-blown pink Roses

Dinner tables at the beginning of Queen Victoria's reign were mainly decorated with food. In the service known as dinner *à la française* dinner guests entered the dining room to find the dishes of the first course spread over the table. When that course had been eaten, the next was brought and set over the table and so it went on. There was a problem with this method of dining. The last dishes to be consumed in each course grew cold. A renowned French chef called Urbain Dubois suggested as a remedy that hostesses adopt a service known as *à la russe*. In this hot dishes were not placed on the table but carved in the kitchen, dished up, brought to the dining room and handed round to guests. The dinner table need not look empty because pastries and dessert fruits could be on it throughout dinner. Fashionable hostesses did adopt this style and added a white tablecloth to set off the fruit. Pastries, however, were relegated to a side table from which it also became the custom to serve all the food.

To avoid the table looking too empty it became the practice to set it with ostentatious-looking epergnes. Their design combined branches for candles, a dish half-way up for fruit and bonbons and a top dish in which the butler put either a sponge cake decorated with flowers or a close, flat arrangement of flowers. A vase well filled with blooms or a large display of fruit decorated with flowers might serve as a centrepiece on the table. This was often flanked by branched candlesticks followed either side by a silver wine cooler containing a well-grown Fuchsia or Geranium. This form of arrangement suited until it began to attract criticism for being heavy. The presence of the epergnes in particular was castigated because they blocked the view and made it difficult for guests facing each other to hold a conversation.

In 1861 Mr March of the Lord Chamberlain's office, St James's Palace, exhibited at a London show an object which could do the job of an epergne but was more light and graceful. It was a vase of his own invention, with a tall glass stem and a glass dish at the base and at the top. His arrangements of fruits and flowers using three of these vases gained him first prize and a considerable amount of public interest. A London firm began to produce the vases, which became known as 'March stands'. Their stems were 24 inches (60 cm) from the tablecloth to the upper glass. This was based on Mr March's calculation that the line of vision of a seated 6-foot (1.8-m) man was 19 inches (48 cm) above the table. The problem of avoiding blocked vision led *The Gardener's Assistant* of 1878 to advise gardeners to provide themselves with a light stick 20 inches (50 cm) long and mark off the point where it reached 15 inches (38 cm). Decorations not higher than 15 inches above the table did not interrupt the sight. On tall vases nothing was to hang below 20 inches (50 cm).

Horizons might have been cleared but the table top became increasingly given over to floral decoration. In addition to central stands or vases it became fashionable for a small glass 'specimen' vase to be put by each place setting. This could contain a Rosebud or a sprig of Stephanotis or similar delicate arrangement. Fingerbowls were ornamented with tufts of flowers dropped into the water and folded tablenapkins might sprout a Rosebud. Flowers, trails of foliage and richly coloured leaves were sometimes laid in patterns on the tablecloth and pieces of Fern and Palm fronds made to radiate from beneath plates.

It was not a trend liked by all. The older generation particularly resented it. One, writing to *The Garden* in 1878, reminisced nostalgically of the days when the chief objects on the table had been dinner and cited the case of a lady of high rank and social influence who drove home from a grand dinner at a neighbour's and ordered mutton chops as 'she had not dined, and could not as both Lady L's flower garden and conservatory seemed crushed on to the table'.

Excesses of table decoration were fuelled by the practice of giving prizes at horticultural shows to those who put up the best exhibits in a class called 'Dinner-table Decorations'. At the Rose Show held at the Crystal Palace in 1870, W. Thomson of Penge set up an extraordinary exhibit. He prepared it by removing the mahogany top from a table and substituting a deal one which had seven holes cut into it. A potted Palm

A drawing-room arbour reconstructed for the television series from an 1874 engraving

was dropped into each hole and a tablecloth consisting of strips of damask laid on. The damask was ironed when it was on the table so that it was perfectly smooth. The Palms with their pots hidden looked as if they were springing out of the tablecloth and, because it was the fashion never to remove the cloth at dinner (previously cloths had been removed before dessert), guests sitting at the display would never guess that they were not dining off mahogany.

This method of display caused a controversy which was to manifest itself in columns of comment in journals for several years. Worried mistresses voiced concern about the desecration of their damask tablecloths and men questioned the naturalness of the style. One critic likened it to taking a picnic in a tropical forest. Although it is reported that this style was used to decorate tables at public dinners, it is not certain how many private dinners were eaten around sunken flower pots. In any case, gardeners who dressed dining tables for their employers had

*Dinner table decorated to an
1874 design*

worries enough without employing the gardens' carpenter to aerate strips of deal. Winter was the most trying time for these gardeners, because a paucity of flowers could coincide with a run of dinner parties two months at a stretch and a change of table decoration be demanded every night. Many head gardeners were disgusted at the waste of flowers and 'hospital accommodation' had to be found for damaged plants brought back to the garden.

Attending to table decoration was also time-consuming. The butler had to be asked the size of the table for the evening; the position of the articles of ornament; whether chandeliers were to be suspended or on the table and how many dishes of dessert were required. The last information was needed so that the gardener could choose dessert fruit and provide glossy or colourful leaves on which to place it. Time had then to be given to thinking up an appropriate decorative scheme for the table, cutting the flowers and overseeing the actual arrangement.

Some decorations could be saved to see another day if they were removed and put into water as soon as dinner guests left the room. *Asparagus plumosus* (introduced from South Africa) turned out to be a blessing in this respect. The delicate Ferny fronds could be used at night without water, and provided that they were put back into water during the day they would last two or three weeks. Bits of Davallia Fern were also durable as they didn't wither and curl up in draughts like other Ferns. If Selaginella (a moss-like plant used to cover the tops of pots) had been lifted with a little earth still attached to its roots, it could be repotted to live on for another day. Considerable amounts of Selaginella were needed and it was grown in any convenient spot. One gardener grew his on the tops of large orange pots in the conservatory.

Above: Pereskia

Right: Pereskia stem with the top split and pieces of Christmas Cactus secured in the split with a Pereskia spine

Left: Method of obtaining a table-top Croton:
(a) top tongued and mossed;
(b) stem showing the tongue;
(c) roots grow from the tongue into the moss

Should flowers be scarce in winter a gardener could make use of the colourful tops of Croton plants. This form of decoration needed preparation. Crotons with suitably handsome tops would be selected and a cut made half-way through the stem. The cut was wedged open and the place bound round with damp moss or a quantity of sandy soil. If the plant was kept warm and moist, roots would form into the moss and the top could be taken off and potted into a 4-inch (10-cm) pot suitable for table decoration. This method echoed the one Harry had used to shorten the Tree Fern in the show house.

Lengthening as well as shortening could also supply winter table decoration. The Christmas Cactus has a naturally sprawling habit but it could be made to grow tall. The method of doing this was to graft it on to a long stem of another kind of Cactus. The favourite root stock was *Pereskia aculeata*. Cuts were made at the top of a 2-foot (60-cm)-tall stem of Pereskia and pieces of Christmas Cactus inserted into them, each stuck firmly in place with a long thorn. The transformation of a Christmas Cactus from a squat to a tall plant in this way is a long-term project. To get a good head you have to wait anything from two to five years. However, once fully developed and in flower, this novelty must have taken pride of place in many a Victorian room.

CHAPTER SIXTEEN
Town and Parlour Gardening

*Suburban lady gardeners – George and Rosa, a newly married couple –
Town gardens – Windowsill and parlour gardening, including a garden
on a mantelpiece.*

Victorian times saw the rise of a new layer of society. Its members, being neither poor nor aristocratic, became known as the 'middle-classes'. They were manufacturers, merchants and professional men who had grown rich from the benefits brought by the Industrial Revolution. To suit their status and as a good investment many middle-class men had 'villa'-type residences built on the outskirts of cities. This gave them a pleasant environment in which to live but was still close enough to the city so that they could travel, often by the new train services, to their businesses.

With their menfolk away at business all day it was often the women of the house who looked after the garden. The size of villa gardens varied, they could be ½ acre (0.2 hectare) or more. Whatever their extent it helped if a part-time gardener or a full-time labourer were employed. With servants to look after children, meals and housework, the ladies themselves could often find time to undertake light gardening tasks. These activities were no doubt increased if they read of the benefits which the writer Mrs Harriet Beecher Stowe thought gardening brought. She believed that stirring the soil and sniffing the morning air gave ladies 'freshness and beauty of cheek and brightness of eye, cheerfulness of temper, vigour of mind, and purity of heart'.

John Loudon had also seen ladies as potential gardeners. In 1838 his book *The Suburban Garden and Villa Gardeners* had been aimed in part at teaching them to lay out a flower garden. Loudon thought that this skill was within the capacity of every woman who could cut out and put together parts of female dress. Two years later his wife, Jane, wrote a series of concise and beautifully illustrated books called *The Ladies' Flower-Garden*. Each volume was devoted to a different category of plants. Her first book described *Ornamental Annuals*. She wrote that the sowing of these, the watering of the seedlings, transplanting, training, cutting-off of dead flowers and gathering of seeds for the following year's crop were all suitable 'feminine occupations'. That they gave gentle exercise in the open air was an additional advantage. As all this cultivation could be carried out within six or eight months. Mrs Loudon also saw annuals as suitable for suburban houses which were being hired for no more than a year.

Manufacturers were not slow to identify a new market in suburban lady gardeners. Advertisements for lawn mowers appeared with the wording 'suitable for a Lady' or with an illustration of a lady pushing a mower. There is no doubt that even the frailest of creatures could have managed the neat little mowers which had cutting blades of just 6 inches (15 cm) in length. These were designed to trim thin strips of grass which margined flower beds or paths. Less manageable were some sets of garden tools specially made for ladies. Their pretty design did nothing to alleviate the fact that, because they were made of iron instead of steel, soil stuck to them and made them too heavy to handle.

Soil itself could be a problem. Some builders who constructed villas in the suburbs of London scooped up and carted away up to 5 feet (1.5 m) in depth from each garden. The clay soil went for brick making. New owners found that they had a garden 5 feet lower than the house and with very poor soil. Advice on what to do in this sort of dilemma and help on other gardening matters could be found in the pages of a magazine entitled the *Villa Gardener*, which first appeared in March 1870. In the May edition readers are introduced to a newly married couple, George and Rosa Merchant Prince, who buy a new villa in Liverpool. After his first night in Mentone Villa, Mount Pleasant Road, George, departing for the office, steps out and sinks knee-deep into snow, mud and water. Fortuitously that evening on his return journey he pops into a stationers and buys the *Villa Gardener*. Edition 1, of course, tells him how to lay out paths. From then on George and Rosa's experiences as they follow advice given in the magazine are recorded each month with George occasionally making such significant statements as: 'It is quite possible that we may be instructed how to make our villa garden a perfect paradise of beauty.' Interestingly, the rather incestuous arrangement of having George and Rosa's garden experiences chronicled in the very same magazine on which they based their garden techniques did not seem to worry its readers. The only adverse criticism received came in February 1871 when a reader wrote to say that he thought that the affection the young couple showed for each other was 'exceeding ordinary bounds'.

E. S. Delamer, writing in about 1860 in *The Flower Garden*, had sensible advice for villa gardeners. He recommended that those who moved into a previously occupied dwelling should wait twelve months to see what was in the garden before attempting to change it. For those starting

Previous page: Detail from All A-Blowing and A-Glowing *by Mary Hayllar*

Suitable 'feminine occupations'

from scratch he advocated 'unity of design', not a 'chance-medley'. In his opinion a winter garden of evergreens mixed with flowers like Hollyhocks, Peonies and Dahlias which died down in the winter was 'very eligible'. In addition a few flower beds could hold Geraniums and Verbena during the summer and from November to March be filled with Chrysanthemums, Pinks, Heliotrope, Forget-me-Nots, Christmas Roses, *Erica carnea* and spring-flowering bulbs together with Russian and Neapolitan Violets and Wallflowers. Delamer also suggests China Roses, but another contemporary source states that it is safe to plant Roses in a suburban garden only if nearby Elms, Poplars, Limes and Willow trees thrive!

If it was risky to plant Roses in a suburban garden it was foolish to do so in a town garden. Smoke and sulphur in the atmosphere made them sickly. Town dwellers foolhardy enough to want standard Roses were advised to replace them every second year with fresh ones and use the old ones as garden canes.

To ensure successful cultivation of any flowers in town gardens Victorian manuals recommend carting away existing soil, which is likely to be exhausted through lack of manure and poisoned by pollution, and substituting fresh, pure soil from a heath or meadow. Those who planted shrubs ran the risk of them being 'drawn up' and becoming weak and drooping through lack of light and air. Some Rhododendrons withstood smoke better than most. Of flowers, it was found that Thrift and London Pride were difficult to kill and Lily-of-the-Valley also did well. Carnations, which in the ordinary course of events were given soot as a manure, flourished but had to be covered over when they were in bloom to stop them being spotted with sooty acid rainwater. Delicate Orchids due to open in winter when fog and smoke were at their worst, could be retarded by being kept cool and made to bloom instead in April. Strong Ferns could be counted on to thrive. Climbers which bore town air well

Above: A suburban garden providing a useful backcloth for a photograph of the whole household at fruit-gathering time

Right: Detail from The Arrival *by Edward Killingworth Johnson (1825–1923)*

were: Blue Passion Flower, white and yellow Jasmine, some Clematis, the Everlasting Pea, the Sweet Pea 'Painted Lady' and Nasturtiums. Flowers such as Sweet William, Canterbury Bells, Stocks, Antirrhinums, Marigolds, Candytuft and Phlox were raised in the country and brought to the town in March. Dahlias, Hollyhocks and Peonies were thought to be suitable only for large gardens.

Most small town gardens had a front and back plot. In the front a popular arrangement was a central bed and one continuous border. Both could be filled with annuals and herbaceous plants and the central bed might have a flowering shrub in the middle. A few evergreens near the house protected it from dust and its inmates from prying eyes. In country towns the back garden could be laid out to look like a small rustic landscape enhanced by 'peeps' of the distant open country, but for gardens in built-up areas a more formal arrangement was considered best. E. S. Delamer suggests small, regular, corresponding beds kept gay by flowers in masses. Spring-flowering bulbs and Lilies were particularly useful for the purpose.

Above: Jasmine

It became fashionable to spread spent tanners' bark on to beds. This gave them a rich chocolate-brown colour which contrasted well with bright bedding plants. Anyone looking for other ideas to enhance their gardens was advised that valuable hints could be obtained from a visit to the public park.

Below: Winter windowbox decorated with evergreens

Near city centres many people had no gardens. The opening of new streets, laying-out of squares and speculative building had taken up all available land. Lack of gardens did not mean, however, that people did not garden; far from it. Local societies organised by clergymen encouraged the poor to grow plants on their windowsills and enter them in competitions. Well-meaning speakers gave talks in school halls advising how this could best be done and discouraged would-be entrants from smartening up flower pots with a coat of bright red paint. Those who could not afford pots, painted or otherwise, used tin cans with holes punched through the bottom.

For the better-off, gardening without a garden was more complex. It fell into two categories: indoor and outdoor.

Outdoor at its simplest was pots of plants on a windowsill – perhaps Calceolarias, Geraniums or Ericas bought from hawkers who carried baskets of them around the streets in late February and March. Hawkers'

plants had, however, a large failure rate. Those which had come straight from a warm glasshouse became chilled as they were carried round; others, like Stocks and Asters, might have been stuck in a pot only an hour before being sold. House owners who lived in central London fared better if they could purchase plants direct from Covent Garden Market. Women porters would, for a small sum, carry boxes any reasonable distance. Fuchsias were favourite sill plants, and so was Mignonette. One writer found the perfume of the latter so powerful in some of 'the better streets' that it was considered 'sufficient to protect the inhabitants from those effluvia which bring disorders with them in the air'. Pots of Musk also scented the atmosphere. Musk was a very useful plant to both grower and recipient. Florists used it to fill up spaces between larger pots and so make up a full load on wagons bound for the city. On windowsills it was known to grow 'under much sufferance'. Sadly and inexplicably Musk lost its perfume at the beginning of the twentieth century.

To cut down on watering, windowsill pots could be dropped into larger ones and the space between the two packed with wet moss. This helped stop evaporation. Plain glass milk-pans, soup-plates, large saucers, zinc dishes and trays and boxes or jardinières could all be pressed into service as containers for (as the *Journal of Horticulture and Cottage Gardener* of December 1861 put it) 'a lovely little spring garden'. Windowboxes made neater containers for plants. Home-made ones could be smartened up by tacking split hazel branches into a pattern across the front or sliding patterned tiles in a row between two thin pieces of wood also attached to the front.

Balconies could be turned into gardens provided it could first be ascertained that they were strong enough. Professionals might have to be called in to advise on this. To help provide an answer as to how much weight it was intended the balcony should hold, a query bound to arise, Cassell's *Popular Gardening* published weights of various-sized pots, with and without soil. Unsafe balconies could be rendered garden-worthy by erecting iron pillar props. These could be disguised with ornamental climbers. In summer flower pots might be filled with colourful annuals and in winter with evergreen shrubs. Miniature balconies which were fitted round windows and held just a few flower pots were known as 'balconettes'. Well-furnished balconies in Park Lane and Piccadilly in London were seen as an education to those who went to look at them. The idea of education was further linked with this sort of gardening, for F. W. Burbidge wrote in *Domestic Floriculture*: 'By growing flowers in our windows we contribute towards the education and refinement of society at large.'

One other form of outdoor window gardening was partly indoors. It took place in a 'conservatory window'. This was a glass case built on to the outside of the bottom half of a sash window. With only half the window covered, light and air could still enter the room. Access to the 'conservatory' was gained by throwing up the lower sash and leaning out. The conservatory base, made of wood and lined with metal, could be filled with earth and planted up with foliage plants and Ferns. Pots of flowering plants might be popped in to brighten up the display. Venetian blinds kept from touching the glass by three vertical wires warded off extremes of heat and cold. In summer the blinds needed to be pulled down for only a few hours but in winter they might have to stay down for a fortnight at a time. In severe weather it was also advisable to burn a candle or a spirit lamp inside the case to keep out frost. Few 'conservatory windows' have survived, but there is one on the outside of Number 18 Stafford Terrace, just off Kensington High Street in London. The house, once the home of Linley Sambourne, a Victorian cartoonist for the magazine *Punch*, is now looked after by The Victorian Society.

Indoor horticulture was also known as 'parlour gardening'. Various magazines gave columns of advice headed 'The Parlour Gardener' which were directed at men whose 'burden of business' forbade them taking a residence in the country, at women obliged to stay in the city because of their families, and at invalids. Parlour gardening was a multifarious occupation. It could entail flower boxes being made up and placed in the window recesses of each room, the design of each box changing with the room – for instance, the box in the parlour could look more 'rustic' than

A rustic parlour box and a more elaborate version for the dining room

Hanging basket

the one in the dining room. Then there was the placing of pots of plants along the centre bar where the window sashes met; beneficial to the plants but considered by some a rather vulgar practice.

Hanging baskets had to be purchased or made. For those who took the latter course a 'natural' basket could be fashioned by hollowing out the base of a large turnip or beetroot and filling it with a Hyacinth bulb and moss. The bulb would grow and the turnip (or beet) sprout fresh young leaves from its crown which would curl decoratively up the sides.

An odd corner of the room might lend itself to 'the Flower-Stand Garden'. This structure, if pushed against a wall, could support a fan-shaped trellis which would form a useful scrambling ground for a pot of Clematis. In the centre of the stand a Camellia looked well, flanked by some pots of Mignonette. The scent of Mignonette was acceptable; anything heavier inside a room was not. *Lilium auratum* was particularly bad, it being said that one flower could fill a room with such powerful perfume that few people could not remain in it long.

Wall space might be given over to 'the Etagère Garden', a series of shelves for potted plants. The shelves were attached to the wall or supported on legs.

'Mantelpiece gardening' started in September when fires were lit. It best suited flowering bulbs which benefited from the fire heat. Mantelpiece gardeners, uncertain as to what bulbs would make a good display in respect of colour, height and time of flowering, could purchase a specially selected package from the bulb specialists Messrs Barr & Sugden. One interesting oddity a 'Parlour Gardener' column suggests for mantelpiece culture is blooming Hyacinths under water. This entails the purchase of two specially-made, plain, uncoloured-glass vases. One had no bottom and into this a Hyacinth bulb was to be placed upside down with a mixture of leaf mould crumbled over it until the vase was three quarters full. A second bulb, whose flower colour would be a good contrast to the first, was to be placed at the top of the vase but, this time, the right way up. This planted-up vase was then stood on top of the other vase which had first been filled with water. If the earth in the upper vase was kept moist, the Hyacinth in its top would put forth leaves and bloom in the air in the normal way. Meanwhile, the Hyacinth

Far left: An ètagère garden
Below left: Wardian case
Left: A flower-stand garden

below, planted upside down, would also put forth leaves and bloom, it was said, quite as well as its companion, but in the water of the bottom vase. These strange-looking combinations, rather like an hour-glass in appearance, were thought to look well at either end of the mantelpiece, especially if they contained similar couples.

In the middle of the parlour, standing either on a table or on its own stand, might be any one of a number of versions of the Wardian case. The most basic form consisted of a plain glass top with a zinc or copper tray beneath it to catch recycled water. The case might hold Ferns, Mosses and Liverworts, all thought to fare better under cover than in the dry atmosphere of the room. Elaborate cases had an aquarium: that is, a sealed middle section filled with water, fish and water plants, and two end sections holding Ferns or fine-foliaged plants.

Then there were specific 'Fern cases' which allowed their owners to enjoy the charms of a Fern house on a small scale. Fern cases could be enlivened by miniature rocks and 'ruins'. There is an extremely interest-

Miniature ruin built on a looking glass

ing section in a book called *Our Flower Garden – How We Made the Most of It* by H. Allnutt (*circa* 1872) on how to make 'ruins' for Fern cases. The technique involves bits of coke, pieces of slate, cement, cardboard boxes and sections of mirror. Using various combinations of these, gothic arches 7 × 4 inches (17.5 × 10 cm), rocks of varying dimensions, castles and bridges could all be built.

Some cases could be made into Lilliputian stovehouses capable of raising exotic flora. To heat these by gas was complicated; to heat them by oil lamp was risky as the oil might spill or the light go out. The best method of heating was found to be hot water: a moderate-sized watering can was filled with hot water three times a day and its contents poured into a container at the base of the case. A substantial layer of sand on the case floor performed the dual function of protecting the plants' roots and holding the heat even when the water cooled. The inmates of the case could be watered once a fortnight (an engineer's oil can was useful for this), and an upper pane of glass occasionally opened 2 inches (5 cm) to let a little air enter.

Despite a parlour gardener of 1861 describing his case as holding 'Ferns, blue Lobelia, small red Geraniums, Anemones, little Blue bells, Snowdrops and the whitewaxed Cyclamen with their deep rose and purple blotch', cases (particularly ones which worked on the true Wardian principle that condensation alone provided all the moisture) were thought too dank for flower culture. Parlour gardeners who wanted a mix of both flowers and other plants were advised to invest in 'plant cabinets'. These could be quite the grandest of all structures involved in chamber horticulture; in fact, gardeners could walk into them.

Making the cabinet might simply involve a pair of glass doors being placed across a bow-window recess, or the cabinet might be given greater depth by erecting glass walls which projected from a recess a few feet into the room. Heating for the cabinet could be achieved by a row of 1- or 2-inch (2.5- or 5-cm) pipes fed with hot water from the kitchen boiler. The *Villa Gardener*, which ran a column on parlour gardening, described these cabinets as excellent for ladies. It stated that they could withdraw into them, inspect their flowers, plants and climbers, water, tend and dress various plants, 'which is quite a lady-like employment', and be out to do other household duties in twenty minutes.

For some ladies that time limit might have been accurate but other more dedicated indoor gardeners could spend hours at gardening tasks. Taking cuttings and 'striking' them, for example, needed time and attention, although a patent propagating case heated by a spirit lamp was a great help. This case had been invented by Peter Barr (of Daffodil fame). Then there was manure. On balconies, guano (imported bird droppings), plus a shovelful of fresh cow dung or sheep droppings would have to be administered with two or three handfuls of pulverised charcoal to suppress the smell. Fortunately, for inside plants shops sold proprietary brands of manure mixture in sealed cans. Lime which was to be mixed with bone dust first had to be made by calcifying a few oyster shells in the kitchen fire.

Time could be given to experiments in hybridising and attempts at grafting. It also had to be found to take established plants out of the house, lay them on to their sides on paving stones and wash them thoroughly. This operation helped to deter pests but obstinately resident greenfly and red spider might warrant being submerged in a cloud of insecticide expelled from a patent vaporiser. The cloud was achieved by blowing through a mouthpiece on the side of the can. Indoors a less energetic remedy was to burn a cigar or a cigarette. Picking off dead leaves; regularly turning plants so that they were not drawn towards the light and so became lop-sided; labelling; sponging Palms, Ficus and Aspidistras; and watering plants on mantelpieces, stands and shelves, in baskets, brackets and boxes all took time. In fact, it is a wonder that ladies found sufficient leisure to make wax flowers, skeletonise leaves, concoct pot-pourri and, with lamp black, comb and toothbrush, print Fern fronds.

An impressive plant cabinet

CHAPTER SEVENTEEN

Memorial Flowers

Gaudy graves – Suitable suggestions – Plants in churchyards –
The London Necropolis – Miss Etta Close and Queen Victoria's funeral –
Mansion wreaths.

As flowers were finding their way on to tables, upon persons and into parlours, they were also inevitably entering the realms of that great Victorian preoccupation – death.

In 1843 John Loudon wrote that respect for the dead was not generally shown by putting flowers on their graves. By 1863 John Robson, who combined being a garden writer with his job as a head gardener, wrote in one of his columns for the *Journal of Horticulture and Cottage Gardener* that the practice of planting flowers on graves was causing as much angry feeling as the prevailing fashion for sculpture. The latter he had described as 'stone, marble and metallic enormities'. The problem lay with over-doing gaudy flowers. The well-to-do, who might be expected to have refined tastes, could be as bad as anyone. Robson describes a typical wealthy family grave: 'An enclosure containing white stone or marble sculpture is surrounded by ironwork often bronzed or gilded, and through the openings are seen the brightest scarlet Geraniums and yellow Calceolarias that the florist can furnish.' Beauty is in the eye of the beholder, for a few years later the grave of baby Prince Alexander, the third son of the Prince and Princess of Wales, is described by a correspondent as having two edgings of dwarf Geraniums and Verbena and as being 'beautiful'.

Anthericum liliastrum

In 1874 *Domestic Floriculture* suggests that the white Rose 'Aimée Vibert' would look pretty on ironwork surrounding a grave; also that Crocuses of every colour, Tulips, Hyacinths, Narcissus and St Bruno's Lily (*Anthericum liliastrum*) were 'desiderata' for a grave's external border. Edging to the grassy mound could be blue *Scilla sibirica* with Snowdrops planted on the mound. (Snowdrops were favourite churchyard flowers, especially over a child's grave.) Daisies, Primroses, Heartsease, Lily-of-the-Valley, Forget-me-Nots, Saxifrage and Anemones, particularly the blue *Anemone apennina*, are also recommended, with blue-and-white Periwinkles carpeting the ground. For summer the choice widens but abundant flowerers such as *Viola cornuta* and the Mule Pink were thought to be useful, as were white Lilies grown in pots and sunk into the grave's border.

For graves with sufficient room to accommodate them, some sources recommend dwarf Roses and miniature Cypresses and Yews. The evergreens would have been stunted by being grown in flower pots, and plunging the pots into the grave turf kept them that way.

Yucca

If graves were being turned into small gardens, then so was 'God's Acre' surrounding them. A Dorset vicar planted up eighteen beds and a border which encircled his churchyard. In 1878, disappointed that the Roses in them flowered for only three months, he expressed his intention to try to have flowers for at least ten months of the year and wrote to *The Garden* for advice. That magazine frequently carried notes of guidance on churchyard cultivation. Small town and rural churchyards were highlighted for the indiscriminate planting which happened in them because they had no public body to impose restrictions. To counter this *The Garden* suggested in 1879 that shrubs and trees should be grouped or placed in isolated positions by one professional person. Groups of *Macleaya cordata*, which could grow to 9 feet (2.7 m) in height and each have six spikes of elegant flowers, were recommended as suitable plants; also Tritomas, as 'for a striking effect they have no superiors', and tall *Campanula pyramidalis*. Yuccas were seen as excellent grouping plants, as were groups of autumn-flowering Anemones, especially 'Honorine Jobert'. In recommending the Anemones it was echoing their oriental origin, for Robert Fortune had first discovered these among tombs in Shanghai in 1843.

The planting in city churchyards was not above criticism. In 1878 a reader had written to *The Garden* warning of the practice of installing shrubs which were too big: 'I imagine that even the Lilac will produce roots sufficiently strong to disturb graves; and I see in Kensington Churchyard many shrubs which, if left in there, will, after a lapse of twenty years, smother the whole place.'

The vogue for planting up inner-city churchyards was helped by the fact that many had been closed to burials. Their closure had followed revelations in the 1830s and 1840s of the dreadful state they were in. So many people had been interred in them over the years that, according to one report, the soil was: 'so saturated and super-saturated with animal matter that it could no longer properly be called soil.' Gases emitted into the air were known to make mourners queasy as they stood beside open graves and in 1841 two gravediggers at St Botoloph's Churchyard in London were so overcome by concentrated 'effluvia' that they perished as they descended into a grave. In 1850 an Act gave power to the Board of Health to forbid further interments in city churchyards and to provide large cemeteries.

In London the plan was for two large cemeteries, one near Abbey Wood and the other an extension to the existing Kensal Green Cemetery. This scheme foundered and from 1854 onwards most of London's dead were buried at a cemetery called the London Necropolis. The cemetery, owned by the London Necropolis Company encompassed 500 acres (202 hectares) of heathland at Brookwood near Woking and was laid out with shrubs, coniferous trees and curving paths. Greenhouses at the cemetery provided shrubs and flowers to those wishing to decorate graves themselves, or for set fees Necropolis employees would each year plant spring bulbs and summer flowers on graves. An extraordinary feature of the Necropolis was its railway. There was a station in the south of the cemetery and one in the north. Arriving at these were trains pulling 'hearse vans' which had been loaded at the company's station in central London. Coffins could travel first, second or third class.

Now simply known as Brookwood Cemetery, the burial ground is today very much in use and is still privately owned. The greenhouses are, alas, decayed and pressures of maintenance have meant that the niceties of being able to offer a private grave-planting service have long since ceased to exist. There are, however, some fine examples of memorials with enduring floral decorations, most of them bearing dates from the last decade of the nineteenth century. They are swathed with carved Roses, *Lilium longiflorum*, Passion Flowers, Ivy and Ferns.

Manners and Tone of Good Society (1875) is exact about periods of mourning: for instance, six weeks was appropriate for a first cousin, two months for an aunt or uncle. It is also informative about wreaths. Relatives and friends could send wreaths of immortelles (these were usually the yellow Helichrysum) and wreaths of white flowers to the house prior to the funeral. For those with close links to the deceased, floral tributes appear to have been more fulsome. *Domestic Floriculture* mentions strewing flowers in the chamber of death or laying them in the coffin. When Queen Victoria died at Osborne on 22 January 1901, the royal ladies put Lilies and white Orchids around her on the death bed. The artist H. von Herkomer recorded the scene and the painting hangs in the Queen's bedroom at Osborne. The funeral ceremony lasted three days, for the coffin had to be brought from the Isle of Wight to Portsmouth and from there to Windsor before finally being placed in the sarcophagus at Frogmore. It began its journey from Osborne on Friday, 1 February.

Above: Carved Passion Flowers cover a memorial at Brookwood Cemetery

Left: Frontispiece from Flower Emblems or The Seasons of Life

FLOWER EMBLEMS

OR

THE SEASONS OF LIFE.

SELECTIONS IN PROSE AND VERSE FROM VARIOUS AUTHORS.

WITH TWELVE COLOURED ILLUSTRATIONS.

MAN COMETH FORTH LIKE A FLOWER

SEELEY, JACKSON, AND HALLIDAY, 54 FLEET STREET.
LONDON.   MDCCCLXXI.

Queen Victoria on her deathbed painted by H. von Herkomer

In the intervening days between the announcement of death and the coffin's arrival in London, Miss Etta Close of 101 Eaton Square had been very busy. She had originated a movement for attaching mourning wreaths to lamp posts and a depot to receive them was opened at 7 Upper Belgrave Street. Miss Close wrote to the *Graphic*:

> I shall be glad if you will mention the extraordinary and touching response the people have made to my appeal for wreaths for the funeral on Saturday. Hundreds have already arrived, sent by the highest and by the very lowest of the land, some of whom carried theirs many miles.

In addition to lamp-post wreaths, floral tributes arrived by the wagon load at Dean's Cloisters. Some of these when unpacked were so wide that it was difficult to get them through the doorway. They came from such disparate bodies as foreign dignitaries, military establishments, institutes (such as the Institute of Journalism) and organisations like Trinity House, which sent a 5-foot-6-inch (1.67-m)-high lighthouse made of Lilies, Carnations and Camellias, with Violets for the lighthouse window. Each city council or corporation sent a tribute too. Reading ordered its wreath from Sutton & Sons (the royal seed establishment), and on the morning of 31 January Suttons displayed it for fifteen minutes so that workers could assemble in admiration.

These wreaths, grand, flamboyant public statements for a monarch as the century turned, were a far cry from the tributes to ordinary mortals. Cost had probably been a minor consideration in their construction, but for families with little money (even less if the deceased had been a breadwinner), funeral tributes were expensive articles. In the country, where wages were low, those with gardens could pick their own flowers. Workers on country estates might have an extra perk. Often, through an understanding with the owner, they could go to the mansion gardens and ask the head gardener to make up their wreaths. They might take their own flowers but could, if they wanted, have flowers from the mansion. They paid a nominal sum for the wire and wreath foundation.

It was by this arrangement that Harry first came into wreath making. Uncle Fred at Blackmoor was often asked to make wreaths, for the nearest florist was at Liss or Petersfield, too great a distance for most people to travel. It was Harry's job to collect moss to tie on to the foundation, and he had to pick every twig out of it; this was something that Uncle Fred had been very particular about. Harry also had to wire the flowers ready for his uncle. At first Uncle Fred used the flowers faster than Harry could wire them, but as the latter became more proficient they had a working system, using pots filled with sand. Harry stood the wired flowers one sort to a pot, so that when needed they could easily be picked out. It is a system he still believes in, especially if making up a wreath without help as he says he's done many times. He believes it is much better to wire up first all the flowers you think you'll need than have to keep stopping to wire them as you go along.

At his present estate moss is not so plentiful as it was down in Hampshire. The best time for it is from round about October until April, and is what Harry calls 'stinging-nettle moss' because it will grow well under a batch of nettles. In his time it was part of Harry's duties to make wreaths for the family who employed him, not only for funerals but also each Christmas and Easter to decorate the family memorial in the village church. The work was never undertaken as a chore; it was, Harry says, considered a great honour and a privilege for the gardener.

BIBLIOGRAPHY

.

BOOKS

Allnutt, H. *Our Flower Garden – How We Made the Most of It* London Estates Office, *c.*1872.

Anderson, A. W. *The Coming of the Flowers* The Country Book Club, 1952.

*Auctarium of the Botanic Gardens, c.*1840.

Baines, T. *Greenhouse & Stove Plants* John Murray, 1885.

The Best of Everything Frederick Warne & Co., *c.*1875.

Birkenhead, J. *Ferns and Fern Culture* J. Birkenhead, 1897.

Book of the Household The London Printing & Publishing Co., *c.*1865.

Bourne, Revd S. E. *The Book of the Daffodil* John Lane: The Bodley Head, *c.*1910.

Boyle, Frederick *The Woodland Orchids* Macmillan & Co. Ltd, 1901.

Bright, Henry A. *The English Flower Garden* Macmillan & Co., 1881.

Burberry, H. A. *The Amateur Orchid Cultivator's Guide Book* Blake & MacKenzie, 1895.

Burbidge, F. W. *Domestic Floriculture* William Blackwood & Son, 1874.

Chittenden, F. J. *Rock Gardens and Rock Plants* Royal Horticultural Society, 1936.

Clarke, John M. *The Brookwood Necropolis Railway* Oakwood Press, 1988.

Darwin, Charles *Insectivorous Plants* John Murray, 1888 (second edition).

Delamer, E. S. *The Flower Garden* George Routledge & Sons, *c.*1860.

Douglas, James *Hardy Florists' Flowers* Pub. James Douglas, 1880.

Flowers From Many Lands Religious Tract Society, *c.*1875.

Francis, G. W. *An Analysis of the British Ferns and their Allies* Simpkin, Marshall & Co., 1855.

Glenny, George *Glenny's Hand-Book of Practical Gardening* C. Cox, *c.*1852.

Heath, Francis George *Where to Find Ferns* Society for Promoting Christian Knowledge, 1885.

Hibberd, Shirley *The Amateur's Flower Garden* Groombridge & Sons, 1878.

Hibberd, Shirley *The Amateur's Greenhouse and Conservatory* Groombridge & Sons, 1888.

Hole, S. Reynolds *A Book About Roses* William Blackwood & Son, 1874.

Hole, S. Reynolds, *Our Gardens* J. M. Dent & Co., 1907.

Hooper's Gardening Guide H. M. Pollett & Co., *c.* 1896.

Household Guide Cassell, Petter and Galpin, *c.*1870.

Language and Poetry of Flowers Milner & Co. Ltd, *c.* 1890.

Loudon, Jane *The Ladies' Flower-Garden (Ornamental Annuals)* Nelson, 1840.

Loudon, Jane *Ladies' Companion to the Flower-Garden* William Smith, 1844.

Loudon, Jane *Practical Instructions in Gardening for Ladies* John Murray, 1841.

Loudon, Jane *The Amateur Gardener* (revised and edited by W. Robinson) Frederick Warne & Co., *c.*1870.

Loudon, John *An Encyclopaedia of Gardening* Longman, Rees, Orme, Brown, Green & Longman, 1834 edition.

Manners and Tone of Good Society or Solecisms to be avoided by a Member of the Aristocracy   Frederick Warne & Co., *c.*1875.

Molyneaux, Edwin *Chrysanthemums and their Culture* Edwin Molyneaux, 1886.

Nicholson, George *The Illustrated Dictionary of Gardening – An Encyclopaedia of Horticulture* Upcott Gill, 1884.

Popular Gardening Volumes 1–4, Cassell & Co. Ltd, 1880.

Robinson, William *Alpine Flowers* John Murray, 1870.

Robinson, William *God's Acre Beautiful – or Cemeteries of the Future* Garden Office, London, 1880.
Robinson, William *The English Flower Garden* John Murray, 1883.
Shaw, C. W. *London Market Gardens* Garden Office, London, 1880.
Sutherland, William *Hardy Herbaceous and Alpine Flowers* William Blackwood & Son, 1871.
Taylor, George M. *Lilies For the Beginner* Garden Book Club, 1947.
Thompson, Robert *The Gardener's Assistant* Blackie & Son, 1859 and 1878 editions.
Thomson, David *Thomson's Handy Book of the Flower Garden* William Blackwood & Sons, 1868 and 1887 editions.
Veitch, James H. *Hortus Veitchii* James H. Veitch, 1906.
Wallace, Dr A. *Notes on Lilies and their Culture* New Plant & Bulb Company, 1879 (second edition).
Weguelin, W. H. *Carnations and Picotees* George Newnes Ltd, 1900.
Wood, Samuel *The Forcing Garden* Crosby Lockwood & Co., 1881.
Wright, John *The Flower Grower's Guide* Volumes 1–6, J. S. Virtue & Co., 1895.
Wright, Walter P. *A Book About Sweet Peas* Headley Brothers, 1912.

VICTORIAN JOURNALS AND PERIODICALS
The Cottage Gardener and Country Gentleman, various editions between 1850 and 1863.
The Floral World and Garden Guide, 1868.
The Gardener, 1867 and 1869, and *The Garden* various editions between 1874 and 1880.
The Gardener's Chronicle, 1870.
The Graphic, June 1874 and February 1901.
The Illustrated London News, March 1870.
The Journal of Horticulture and Cottage Gardener, various editions between 1868 and 1875.
The Quarterly Review, 1842.
The Villa Gardener, March 1870 to March 1871.

PICTURE CREDITS

.

INDEX